EDITOR: Maryanne Blacker

FOOD EDITOR: Pamela Clark

DESIGN DIRECTOR: Neil Carlyle

• • •

ASSISTANT FOOD EDITORS:
Jan Castorina, Karen Green

ASSOCIATE FOOD EDITOR: Enid Morrison

CHIEF HOME ECONOMIST: Kathy Wharton

HOME ECONOMISTS: Jane Ash, Tikki Durrant,
Sue Hipwell, Karen Hughes, Tracey Kern,
Quinton Kohler, Jill Lange, Voula Mantzouridis,
Alexandra McCowan, Kathy McGarry,
Louise Patniotis, Dimitra Stais

PHOTOGRAPHERS: Bruce Allan, Kevin Brown,
Robert Clark, Andre Martin, Robert Taylor,
Jon Waddy

FOOD STYLISTS: Marie-Helene Clauzon,
Rosemary de Santis, Carolyn Fienberg,
Michelle Gorry, Jacqui Hing, Anna Phillips,
Kathy Wharton

EDITORIAL ASSISTANT: Elizabeth Gray

KITCHEN ASSISTANT: Amy Wong

• • •

HOME LIBRARY STAFF:

ASSISTANT EDITOR: Judy Newman

SUB-EDITOR: Danielle Farah

ART DIRECTOR: Robbylee Phelan

CADET ARTIST: Louise McGeachie

SECRETARY: Wendy Moore

• • •

PUBLISHER: Richard Walsh

DEPUTY PUBLISHER: Graham Lawrence

• • •

Produced by The Australian Women's Weekly
Home Library
Typeset by Letter Perfect, Sydney.
Printed by Dai Nippon Co Ltd, Tokyo, Japan.
Published by Australian Consolidated Press,
54 Park Street Sydney
Distributed by Network Distribution Company,
54 Park Street Sydney
Distributed in the U.K. by Australian Consolidated Press (UK)
Ltd (0604) 760 456. Distributed in Canada
by Whitecap Books Ltd (604) 980 9852. Distributed in South
Africa by Intermag (011) 493 3200.

• • •

Biscuits and Slices.
Includes index.
ISBN 0 949128 24 4.

1. Cake. 2. Cookies. (Series: Australian
Women's Weekly Home Library).

641.8653

• • •

OUR COVER: Raspberry Coconut Rings,
page 98, Pecan Shortbreads, page 32, Sour Cream and Lemon
Shortbreads, page 37, Almond Honey Bars, page 26.
PICTURE OPPOSITE: Caramel, Date
and Walnut Slice, page 85.
BACK COVER: Chocolate Peppermint Cookies,
Crunchy Carob Biscuits, Chocolate Fudge Cookies, page 2.

Biscuits & Slices

Home-made biscuits, cookies and slices have special appeal
with their tempting aromas and flavours. Some of our sweet
ones are splendidly rich; others are simpler but no less
delicious. There's a savoury section, as well, with lots of tasty
bites to enjoy. See below for a guide to the sections or check
for your favourite flavours in our fast-find index, starting on
page 126. First though, it's worth taking time to read our Hints
for Success at the back of this book.

Pamela Clark

FOOD EDITOR

BRITISH & NORTH AMERICAN READERS Please note conversion charts for cup and spoon
measurements and oven temperatures are on page 126.

CHOCOLATE, COFFEE AND CAROB

Smooth chocolate, chunky chocolate, lots and lots of chocolate, carob, coffee and mocha treats are all here for your pleasure, in sweet delights to serve after dinner or at any time. If you don't like carob, use chocolate and cocoa in equivalent amounts to carob and carob powder quantities in recipes. You can also use the same amount of dry instant coffee for coffee substitute. First, though, turn to the back of this book for our useful "Hints for Success" section.

CRUNCHY CAROB COOKIES

1¼ cups plain flour
½ cup icing sugar
2 tablespoons light carob powder
125g butter
1 cup (110g) packaged ground
   hazelnuts
1 egg yolk
CRUNCHY TOPPING
150g carob, melted
100g butter, melted
1 tablespoon packaged ground
   hazelnuts
1½ cups (45g) Rice Bubbles

Sift dry ingredients into bowl, rub in butter. Stir in hazelnuts and egg yolk, mix to a firm dough. Turn dough onto lightly floured surface, knead until smooth; cover, refrigerate for 30 minutes.
   Roll dough between sheets of greaseproof paper until 5mm thick. Cut 5cm rounds from dough, place rounds about 3cm apart on greased oven trays. Bake in moderately hot oven for about 10 minutes or until lightly browned; cool on trays. Drop about 2 level teaspoons of topping onto each biscuit, refrigerate until set.
Crunchy Topping: Combine all ingredients in bowl.
   Makes about 35.

CHOCOLATE PEPPERMINT COOKIES

125g butter
180g dark chocolate, chopped
¼ cup brown sugar
¼ cup light corn syrup
1 egg, lightly beaten
1¼ cups plain flour
¼ cup self-raising flour
100g hard peppermint boiled sweets,
   roughly crushed

Combine butter, chocolate, sugar and corn syrup in pan, stir over heat until smooth, stand for 5 minutes. Stir in egg and sifted flours; cover mixture, refrigerate for 1 hour.
   Roll 2 level teaspoons of mixture into a ball, place onto greased oven tray. Repeat with remaining mixture, allowing about 5cm between cookies. Press sweets gently onto each cookie. Bake in moderate oven for about 6 minutes or until firm. Stand cookies on trays for 5 minutes before lifting onto wire racks to cool.
   Makes about 50.

CHOCOLATE FUDGE COOKIES

2 eggs
¼ cup brown sugar
180g dark chocolate, melted
½ cup oil
1¼ cups plain flour
¼ cup self-raising flour
100g white chocolate, roughly
   chopped
1 cup (190g) Choc Bits

Beat eggs and sugar in small bowl with electric mixer until frothy. Stir in combined cooled dark chocolate and oil, then sifted flours, white chocolate and Choc Bits; cover, refrigerate for 1 hour.
   Roll 1½ level tablespoons of mixture into a ball, place onto greased oven tray. Repeat with remaining mixture, allowing about 4cm between cookies. Bake in moderate oven for about 10 minutes or until just firm, cool on trays.
   Makes about 20.

RIGHT: In basket from left: Chocolate Peppermint Cookies, Crunchy Carob Cookies, Chocolate Fudge Cookies.

COFFEE DATE SCROLLS

90g butter
⅓ cup castor sugar
2 teaspoons dry instant coffee
1 teaspoon hot water
2 egg yolks
1⅓ cups plain flour
icing sugar

DATE FILLING
¾ cup chopped dates
⅓ cup water
1 tablespoon dark rum
¾ cup packaged ground almonds

Beat butter and sugar in small bowl with electric mixer until light and fluffy, beat in combined coffee and water. Add egg yolks, beat until combined. Stir in sifted flour, knead dough on lightly floured surface until smooth; cover, refrigerate for 30 minutes.

Roll dough between sheets of greaseproof paper to 25cm x 30cm rectangle. Spread evenly with cold filling, roll up dough from long sides to meet in centre; cover, refrigerate for 30 minutes.

Cut roll into 3mm slices, place onto greased oven trays about 3cm apart. Bake in moderately hot oven for about 12 minutes or until lightly browned. Stand for 5 minutes before lifting onto wire racks to cool. Dust with sifted icing sugar.
Date Filling: Combine dates, water and rum in pan, bring to boil, simmer, uncovered, for about 5 minutes or until mixture is thick and pulpy. Blend or process mixture until smooth. Stir in nuts; cool.

Makes about 50.

CHOCOLATE PEANUTTIES

125g butter, melted
1 teaspoon vanilla essence
½ cup castor sugar
1 egg
1¼ cups self-raising flour
2 tablespoons cocoa
¾ cup chopped unsalted roasted peanuts
1 cup (150g) finely chopped unsalted roasted peanuts, extra

Beat butter, essence, sugar and egg in bowl until smooth. Stir in sifted flour and cocoa, then chopped nuts.

Roll 2 level teaspoons of mixture into a ball, roll in extra nuts, place on greased oven tray; flatten slightly. Repeat with remaining mixture, allowing about 5cm between biscuits. Bake in moderate oven for about 15 minutes or until firm. Lift onto wire racks to cool.

Makes about 50.

COFFEE CREAM STARS

3 teaspoons dry instant coffee
1½ teaspoons boiling water
125g butter
¾ cup icing sugar
1 egg
1¼ cups plain flour
1¼ cups self-raising flour
icing sugar, extra
silver cachous

MOCHA CREAM FILLING
2 tablespoons cream
1 teaspoon dry instant coffee
30g butter
100g white chocolate, chopped
2 tablespoons icing sugar

Dissolve coffee and water in cup. Beat butter and sifted icing sugar in small bowl with electric mixer until light and fluffy. Beat in egg and coffee mixture. Transfer mixture to large bowl. Stir in sifted flours in 2 batches. Knead dough on lightly floured surface until smooth; cover, refrigerate for 30 minutes.

Roll dough between sheets of greaseproof paper until 3mm thick. Cut stars from dough using 5cm cutter. Place stars about 2cm apart on greased oven trays. Bake in moderate oven for about 10 minutes or until lightly browned. Lift onto wire racks to cool.

Reserve 2 tablespoons of filling. Spoon remaining filling into piping bag fitted with small plain tube. Pipe filling onto half the biscuits, top with remaining biscuits. Cover half of each biscuit with paper, dust other half with sifted extra icing sugar. Pipe reserved filling onto centres of biscuits, top with cachous.
Mocha Cream Filling: Combine cream, coffee and butter in pan, stir over low heat until coffee is dissolved and butter melted. Remove from heat, add chocolate, stir until melted; stir in sifted icing sugar. Refrigerate until mixture is thick.

Makes about 60.

CHOCOLATE-DIPPED COFFEE CREAM FANCIES

60g butter
1 teaspoon coffee and chicory essence
1½ tablespoons castor sugar
⅔ cup plain flour
1 cup (150g) Choc Melts, melted
COFFEE CREAM
1¼ cups icing sugar
2 teaspoons oil
¼ teaspoon coffee and chicory essence
1 tablespoon milk, approximately

Beat butter, essence and sugar in small bowl with electric mixer until light and fluffy. Stir in sifted flour, mix to a firm dough; cover, refrigerate for 30 minutes.

Roll dough between sheets of greaseproof paper until 3mm thick. Cut 3½cm rounds from dough, place rounds about 2cm apart on greased oven trays. Bake in moderate oven for about 8 minutes or until lightly coloured. Stand biscuits for a few minutes on trays, lift onto wire racks to cool.

Spread biscuits with coffee cream, stand on wire racks until set. Dip biscuits into Choc Melts, stand on foil-covered tray until set.

Coffee Cream: Sift icing sugar into bowl, stir in oil, essence and enough milk to make spreadable.

Makes about 40.

LEFT: Coffee Cream Stars.
ABOVE: Clockwise from left: Coffee Date Scrolls, Chocolate-Dipped Coffee Cream Fancies, Chocolate Peanutties.

China from Mikasa; other accessories from Fossickers Antiques

COFFEE PECAN BISCUITS

½ cup pecans
2 teaspoons dry instant coffee
1 teaspoon hot water
1¼ cups self-raising flour
⅓ cup castor sugar
125g butter
1 egg yolk
2 teaspoons cold water,
    approximately
¾ cup (75g) pecans, extra
COFFEE ICING
1½ cups icing sugar
2 teaspoons soft butter
1 teaspoon dry instant coffee
3 teaspoons hot water

Blend or process nuts until fine. Dissolve coffee and hot water in cup; cool. Sift flour and sugar into bowl, rub in butter. Stir in nuts, egg yolk, coffee mixture and enough cold water to make a soft dough. Turn dough onto lightly floured surface, knead lightly until smooth; cover, refrigerate for 30 minutes.

Roll 2 level teaspoons of mixture into a ball, flatten slightly, place onto greased oven tray. Repeat with remaining mixture, allowing about 4cm between biscuits. Bake in moderate oven for about 15 minutes or until lightly browned. Lift onto wire racks to cool. Spread biscuits with icing, top with extra nuts.
Coffee Icing: Sift icing sugar into bowl, stir in butter and combined coffee and water. Add a little more hot water, if necessary, to make spreadable.

Makes about 40.

MOCHA BROWNIES

180g unsalted butter
250g dark chocolate, chopped
¾ cup castor sugar
1 tablespoon dry instant coffee
1 tablespoon hot water
3 eggs
1½ cups plain flour

Grease deep 19cm square cake pan, cover base with paper, grease paper. Melt butter and chocolate in pan over low heat, stir until smooth. Remove from heat, stir in sugar and combined coffee and water, then eggs 1 at a time. Stir in sifted flour, pour mixture into prepared pan. Bake in moderate oven for about 35 minutes or until firm; cool in pan. Dust with sifted icing sugar, if desired, before serving.

RIGHT: From left: Mocha Brownies, Coffee Pecan Biscuits.

WHITE CHOCOLATE CHUNK BROWNIES

200g dark chocolate, chopped
150g butter
½ cup castor sugar
2 eggs, lightly beaten
2 teaspoons vanilla essence
⅓ cup plain flour
¼ cup self-raising flour
100g white chocolate, chopped
¾ cup pecans or walnuts, chopped

Grease 20cm x 30cm lamington pan, cover base with paper, grease paper. Melt dark chocolate and butter in pan. Remove from heat, stir in sugar, then eggs and essence, then sifted flours, white chocolate and nuts.

Spread mixture into prepared pan, bake in moderate oven for about 35 minutes or until surface is bubbly and slightly puffed. Cool in pan, refrigerate for several hours or overnight before cutting. Dust with a little sifted icing sugar, if desired, before serving.

MOCHA CREAM FINGERS

100g butter
½ cup castor sugar
1 egg
1½ cups plain flour
2 tablespoons cocoa
2 tablespoons custard powder
¼ cup castor sugar, extra
MOCHA CREAM
60g unsalted butter
1¼ cups icing sugar
1 teaspoon dry instant coffee
1 teaspoon cocoa
1 tablespoon boiling water

Beat butter, sugar and egg in small bowl with electric mixer until light and fluffy. Stir in sifted flour, cocoa and custard powder in 2 batches. Turn dough onto lightly floured surface, knead gently until smooth; cover, refrigerate for 30 minutes.

Roll dough between sheets of greaseproof paper until 4mm thick. Cut 3cm x 6cm rectangles from the dough. Place rectangles about 2cm apart on greased oven trays.

Prick each rectangle all over with a fork, sprinkle with extra sugar. Bake in moderate oven for about 12 minutes or until firm; cool on trays. Sandwich cold biscuits with mocha cream.
Mocha Cream: Beat butter in small bowl with electric mixer until creamy, gradually beat in sifted icing sugar and combined coffee, cocoa and water.

Makes about 30.

CHOCOLATE, RUM AND RAISIN SLICE

1 cup (170g) chopped raisins
2 tablespoons dark rum
100g butter, melted
1½ cups (185g) plain chocolate
   biscuit crumbs
1½ cups (45g) Rice Bubbles
1 cup (70g) shredded coconut
400g can sweetened condensed milk

Grease 23cm square slab pan, cover base with paper, grease paper. Combine raisins and rum in bowl; stand for 1 hour.

Pour butter evenly into prepared pan, sprinkle evenly with biscuit crumbs then half the Rice Bubbles. Top with raisin mixture, coconut, then remaining Rice Bubbles. Drizzle evenly with condensed milk. Bake in moderate oven for about 20 minutes or until lightly browned. Cool in pan, refrigerate 1 hour before cutting.

LEFT: White Chocolate Chunk Brownies.
ABOVE: From back: Chocolate, Rum and Raisin Slice, Mocha Cream Fingers.

Left: China from Country Form; cloth from Accoutrement. Above: Coffee grinder, board and plate from The Country Trader.

CAROB PISTACHIO COOKIES

180g butter
1/3 cup castor sugar
1 1/2 cups plain flour
1 tablespoon dark carob powder
1 cup (30g) Rice Bubbles, lightly crushed
1/4 cup coconut, toasted
75g carob, melted
1/3 cup chopped pistachio nuts

Beat butter and sugar in small bowl with electric mixer until light and creamy. Stir in sifted flour and carob powder, then Rice Bubbles and coconut. Roll 2 level teaspoons of mixture into a ball, place onto greased oven tray, flatten slightly. Repeat with remaining mixture, allowing about 3cm between cookies.

Bake in slow oven for about 20 minutes or until lightly coloured; cool on trays. Spread cookies with carob, sprinkle with nuts.

Makes about 40.

FRUITY CRACKLE SLICE

2 cups (60g) Rice Bubbles
1/3 cup mixed peel
1/4 cup currants
1/3 cup flaked almonds, toasted
125g butter, melted
250g white chocolate, melted

Lightly grease 23cm square slab pan, cover base with paper, grease paper. Combine Rice Bubbles, peel, currants and lightly crushed almonds in bowl. Stir in butter and chocolate. Spread mixture into prepared pan; refrigerate until set.

MOCK COFFEE CAROB FINGERS

125g butter
1/2 cup brown sugar, firmly packed
1 egg yolk
2 teaspoons coffee substitute
2 teaspoons boiling water
1 1/4 cups plain flour
2 tablespoons dark carob powder
ICING
1 1/2 cups icing sugar
2 teaspoons coffee substitute
2 tablespoons boiling water

Beat butter, sugar and egg yolk in small bowl with electric mixer until light and fluffy. Stir in combined coffee substitute and water, then sifted dry ingredients. Mix to a soft dough; cover, refrigerate 30 minutes.

Shape 2 level teaspoons of dough into finger shape about 7cm long, place onto greased oven tray. Repeat with remaining dough, allowing about 3cm between fingers. Mark fingers diagonally with knife.

Bake in moderate oven for about 15 minutes, cool on trays. Half-dip biscuits into icing; stand on wire rack until set.
Icing: Sift icing sugar into small bowl, stir in combined coffee substitute and water; stir until smooth.

Makes about 30.

LEFT: Clockwise from back: Fruity Crackle Slice, Carob Pistachio Cookies, Mock Coffee Carob Fingers.

CAROB CREAMS

150g butter
2 tablespoons icing sugar
1 egg yolk
1½ cups plain flour
¼ cup custard powder
2 tablespoons light carob powder
50g carob, grated
CAROB CREAM
150g carob, melted
100g butter, melted

Beat butter, sifted icing sugar and egg yolk in small bowl with electric mixer until light and fluffy. Stir in sifted flour, custard powder and carob powder in 2 batches. Press mixture together firmly with hands, knead on lightly floured surface until smooth; cover, refrigerate for 30 minutes.

Roll dough between sheets of greaseproof paper until 3mm thick. Cut 5cm rounds from dough, place about 3cm apart on greased oven trays. Bake in moderate oven for about 12 minutes or until lightly coloured; cool on trays.

Join biscuits with ½ level teaspoon carob cream, spread edges with a little more cream, roll edges in grated carob.
Carob Cream: Combine carob and butter, cool to room temperature, refrigerate for 10 minutes; beat with spoon until thick and spreadable.

Makes about 25.

DOUBLE CHOCOLATE MARSHMALLOW CREAMS

½ cup plain flour
¼ teaspoon bicarbonate of soda
1 tablespoon cocoa
2 tablespoons castor sugar
½ cup rolled oats
60g butter, melted
1 egg yolk
2 tablespoons Choc Bits
2 teaspoons water, approximately
2 tablespoons finely chopped pecans
  or walnuts
TOPPING
¾ cup (115g) White Melts
50g pink marshmallows
1 tablespoon cream

Sift flour, soda, cocoa and sugar into bowl, stir in oats, butter and egg yolk. Stir in Choc Bits and enough water to make ingredients cling together. Press mixture firmly together with hands.

Roll dough between sheets of greaseproof paper until 5mm thick. Cut into 4cm rounds, place 3cm apart on greased oven trays. Bake in moderate oven for about 12 minutes or until firm; cool on trays. Spread a level teaspoon of topping onto biscuits, sprinkle with nuts.
Topping: Combine all ingredients in top half of double saucepan or in heatproof bowl, stir over hot water until smooth.

Makes about 30.

RIGHT: From left: Double Chocolate Marshmallow Creams, Carob Creams.

CHOCOLATE ORANGE RINGS

125g butter
¾ cup brown sugar, firmly packed
1 egg
1¾ cups plain flour
¼ cup self-raising flour
1⅓ cups (200g) Choc Melts, melted
3 teaspoons oil
½ cup finely chopped pistachio nuts

ORANGE CREAM FILLING
50g butter
1 teaspoon grated orange rind
1 tablespoon milk
2 teaspoons orange juice
¾ cup icing sugar

Beat butter, sugar and egg in small bowl with electric mixer until smooth. Stir in sifted flours in 2 batches. Knead dough on lightly floured surface until smooth; cover, refrigerate for 30 minutes.

Roll dough on lightly floured surface until 3mm thick, cut into 7cm rounds. Cut 3cm centres from each round. Place rings on greased oven trays. Bake in moderate oven for about 12 minutes or until lightly browned. Lift onto wire racks to cool.

Sandwich cold biscuits with filling, dip 1 side of each biscuit in combined Choc Melts and oil, sprinkle with nuts. Place on foil-covered tray until set.

Orange Cream Filling: Beat butter and rind in small bowl with electric mixer until smooth, gradually beat in milk, juice and sifted icing sugar.

Makes about 30.

CHOCOLATE MALT CRISPS

180g butter
1 teaspoon vanilla essence
1 cup castor sugar
¼ cup malted milk powder
1 teaspoon bicarbonate of soda
1 tablespoon cocoa
3 cups plain flour
⅓ cup water
⅓ cup (50g) White Melts, melted
CREAMY MALT FILLING
40g butter
1 cup icing sugar
2 tablespoons malted milk powder
1 tablespoon milk

Beat butter, essence and sugar in small bowl with electric mixer until light and fluffy. Transfer to large bowl. Stir in sifted milk powder, soda, cocoa and flour with the water in 2 batches. Roll level teaspoons of mixture into balls, place about 4cm apart on greased oven trays, press lightly with spatula. Bake in moderately hot oven for about 12 minutes or until lightly coloured. Cool biscuits on trays. Sandwich cold biscuits with filling; drizzle with White Melts.

Creamy Malt Filling: Beat butter until creamy, beat in sifted icing sugar, milk powder and milk.

Makes about 70.

BELOW: From top: Chocolate Orange Rings, Chocolate Malt Crisps.

CHOCOLATE BISCUIT POPS

You will need about 15 Paddle Pop sticks for this recipe.

1 cup (110g) Milo
¼ cup hot milk
250g butter
¼ cup castor sugar
1 egg
2½ cups plain flour
⅔ cup self-raising flour
100g dark chocolate, finely chopped
1 cup (150g) Choc Melts, melted
1 tablespoon oil
1 cup (150g) White Melts, melted
¼ cup crushed mixed nuts

Dissolve Milo in milk in bowl; cool. Beat butter, sugar and egg in small bowl with electric mixer until light and fluffy. Transfer mixture to large bowl, stir in Milo mixture and sifted flours in 2 batches.

Turn mixture onto lightly floured surface, gently knead in chopped chocolate. Roll dough between sheets of greaseproof paper until 1cm thick. Cut dough into shapes about 6cm x 8cm, place about 4cm apart on greased oven trays, insert a stick 3cm into base of each shape. Bake in moderate oven for about 15 minutes or until lightly coloured. Stand biscuits on trays for 5 minutes before lifting onto wire racks to cool.

Combine Choc Melts with half the oil in a cup, dip top third of biscuits into chocolate mixture, place onto greaseproof paper to set. Combine White Melts and remaining oil in cup, dip ends of biscuits into mixture, dip into nuts, place onto greaseproof paper to set.

Makes about 15.

CHOCOLATE NOUGAT SLICE

50g dark chocolate, melted
¼ cup sweetened condensed milk
2 teaspoons brandy
1 cup (125g) plain sweet biscuit crumbs
2 x 70g packets dessert nougat
1 tablespoon milk
⅓ cup (50g) White Melts, chopped
50g dark chocolate, melted, extra
1 teaspoon oil

Line deep 19cm square cake pan with foil. Combine chocolate, condensed milk, brandy and crumbs in bowl; press into prepared pan, refrigerate for 1 hour.

Chop nougat, without peeling away wafer paper. Combine nougat, milk and White Melts in pan, stir over low heat until nougat is melted. Spread mixture quickly over base. Drizzle with combined extra chocolate and oil, refrigerate until set.

LEFT: Chocolate Biscuit Pops.
ABOVE: Chocolate Nougat Slice.

NUTS AND SEEDS

Crunchy morsels of flavour, nuts and seeds also contain good oils that make them high in nutritional value . If you prefer to use your own favourite nuts, substitute an equivalent amount for the quantity given in any of our recipes. However, do not substitute one type of seed for another. And when buying sunflower seed kernels and pepitas (pumpkin seed kernels), be sure to buy kernels, not seeds, otherwise you will find the shells difficult to break open. Now turn to our "Hints for Success" section at the back of this book for more information.

SPICED RASPBERRY ALMONDETTES

1½ cups plain flour
¼ cup icing sugar
1 teaspoon ground cinnamon
½ teaspoon ground ginger
¼ teaspoon ground nutmeg
125g butter
½ cup packaged ground almonds
1 egg yolk
1 tablespoon water, approximately
1 egg white, lightly beaten
½ cup slivered almonds
⅓ cup raspberry jam

Sift flour, icing sugar and spices into bowl, rub in butter; stir in ground almonds. Stir in egg yolk and enough water to mix to a firm dough. Turn dough onto lightly floured surface, knead lightly until smooth; cover, refrigerate for 30 minutes.

Roll dough between sheets of greaseproof paper until 3mm thick. Cut 5cm rounds from dough. Cut 2cm centres from half the rounds.

Place rounds and rings about 2cm apart on greased oven trays. Brush rings with egg white, sprinkle with slivered almonds. Bake in moderately hot oven for about 12 minutes or until lightly browned. Lift biscuits onto wire racks to cool. Spread rounds with jam, top with rings.

Makes about 40.

CRISP SUNFLOWER NUT BREAD

3 egg whites
½ cup castor sugar
1 cup plain flour
⅓ cup pine nuts
⅓ cup unsalted pepitas (pumpkin seed kernels)
⅓ cup sunflower seed kernels
1 tablespoon sesame seeds

Lightly grease 8cm x 26cm bar pan, cover base with paper, grease paper.

Beat egg whites in small bowl with electric mixer until soft peaks form, gradually add sugar, beat until dissolved between each addition. Stir in sifted flour, nuts, kernels and seeds.

Spread mixture into prepared pan. Bake in moderate oven for about 40 minutes or until firm; cool in pan. Wrap bread in foil, stand for 1 to 2 days.

Cut bread into 4mm slices, place slices in single layer on ungreased oven trays, bake in moderate oven for about 12 minutes or until crisp.

Makes about 60.

LEFT: Spiced Raspberry Almondettes.
ABOVE: Crisp Sunflower Nut Bread.

Left: China from Shop 3, Balmain. Above: Shawl from Flossoms

FUDGY CHOC NUT BROWNIES

125g unsalted butter
90g dark chocolate, chopped
90g milk chocolate, chopped
½ cup brown sugar, firmly packed
2 tablespoons honey
2 eggs
1 cup plain flour
**⅔ cup unsalted macadamia nuts,
    chopped**

Grease deep 19cm square cake pan, cover base with paper, grease paper. Melt butter and both chocolates in pan over low heat. Remove from heat, stir in sugar and honey. Stir in eggs 1 at a time, then sifted flour and nuts, pour into prepared pan. Bake in moderate oven for about 30 minutes or until firm. Cool in pan, cut when cold.

PEANUT COCONUT CHIPPERS

This recipe does not contain flour.

400g can sweetened condensed milk
½ cup crunchy peanut butter
2 cups (140g) shredded coconut
**1 cup (75g) lightly crushed
    lightly salted potato crisps**

Combine all ingredients in bowl; mix gently. Place 2 level teaspoons of mixture together on greased oven tray. Repeat with remaining mixture, allowing about 3cm between biscuits. Bake in moderately hot oven for about 8 minutes or until lightly browned; cool on trays.
    Makes about 35.

*RIGHT: From left: Fudgy Choc Nut Brownies,
Peanut Coconut Chippers.*

China from Shop 3, Balmain

NUTTY HONEY DIAMONDS

1 cup plain flour
2 tablespoons castor sugar
60g butter
1 egg yolk
2 tablespoons water, approximately
½ cup (75g) White Melts, melted

TOPPING
1 cup (110g) packaged ground
    hazelnuts
1 cup (120g) packaged ground
    almonds
2 tablespoons honey
2 eggs, lightly beaten

Grease 20cm x 30cm lamington pan. Sift flour and sugar into bowl, rub in butter. Add egg yolk and enough water to mix to a soft dough. Knead dough on lightly floured surface; cover, refrigerate 30 minutes.

Roll dough large enough to line base of prepared pan. Bake in moderately hot oven for about 10 minutes or until lightly browned and firm.

Spread hot base with topping, bake in moderate oven for about further 15 minutes or until topping is firm; cool in pan. Cut when cold; drizzle with White Melts.
Topping: Combine all ingredients in bowl.

CASHEW GINGER FINGERS

125g butter
¼ cup castor sugar
1 cup self-raising flour
1 teaspoon ground ginger

TOPPING
½ cup icing sugar
60g butter
1½ tablespoons golden syrup
1 cup (150g) unsalted roasted
    cashew nuts, chopped
¼ cup finely chopped glace ginger

Lightly grease 20cm x 30cm lamington pan, place strip of paper to cover base and extend over 2 opposite ends, grease paper. Beat butter and sugar in small bowl with electric mixer until light and fluffy, stir in sifted flour and ginger.

Spread mixture evenly over base of prepared pan, bake in moderate oven for about 20 minutes or until lightly browned; cool in pan. Spread hot topping evenly over cold base; cool.
Topping: Combine sifted icing sugar, butter and syrup in pan, stir over heat until butter is melted; stir in nuts and ginger.

ALMOND BISCUITS WITH MANGO CREAM

2 egg whites
½ cup castor sugar
⅓ cup plain flour
60g butter, melted
2 teaspoons mango essence
¼ cup flaked almonds

MANGO CREAM
170g can mango pulp
60g unsalted butter
½ teaspoon mango essence

Lightly grease and flour oven trays. Mark 5cm circles about 2cm apart on trays. Beat egg whites in small bowl with electric mixer until soft peaks form, gradually add sugar, beat until dissolved between each addition. Fold in sifted flour, cooled butter and essence in 2 batches.

Spread 1 teaspoon of mixture evenly into each circle on trays. Sprinkle half the circles with almonds.

Bake in moderate oven for about 6 minutes or until lightly browned around edges. Lift biscuits carefully onto wire racks to cool. When cold, sandwich plain and almond-topped biscuits with a little mango cream. Dust with sifted icing sugar, if desired.
Mango Cream: Bring mango pulp to boil in pan, boil, uncovered, for about 5 minutes or until thick and spreadable, stirring occasionally; cool. Beat butter and essence in small bowl with electric mixer until pale, gradually beat in mango.

Makes about 25.

PEPITA AND SESAME SLICE

90g butter
1 teaspoon grated lemon rind
2 tablespoons castor sugar
1 egg
⅔ cup white plain flour
½ cup wholemeal plain flour
½ cup unsalted pepitas (pumpkin
    seed kernels), chopped
¼ cup apricot jam
2 tablespoons sesame seeds, toasted
2 tablespoons coffee crystals

Grease 23cm square slab pan, place strip of paper to cover base and extend over 2 opposite sides, grease paper. Beat butter, rind, sugar and egg in small bowl with electric mixer until light and fluffy. Stir in sifted flours and pepitas, press mixture evenly into prepared pan.

Spread base with jam, sprinkle with combined seeds and coffee crystals. Bake in moderately hot oven for about 20 minutes or until lightly browned; cool slice in pan.

LEFT: From left: Nutty Honey Diamonds, Cashew Ginger Fingers.
RIGHT: From top: Almond Biscuits with Mango Cream, Pepita and Sesame Slice.

ALMOND AND REDCURRANT KISSES

60g butter
¼ teaspoon almond essence
¼ cup castor sugar
¼ cup packaged ground almonds
⅓ cup plain flour
1 egg white
⅓ cup redcurrant jelly
icing sugar

Beat butter, essence and sugar in small bowl with electric mixer until light and fluffy, stir in almonds and sifted flour. Beat egg white until soft peaks form, fold into mixture in 2 batches.

Drop level teaspoons of mixture about 5cm apart on greased oven trays. Bake in moderate oven for about 6 minutes or until lightly browned. Lift carefully with spatula onto wire racks to cool. Sandwich biscuits with a little warmed jelly. Dust with sifted icing sugar.

Makes about 20.

POPPY SEED AND APRICOT CRESCENTS

125g butter
125g packet cream cheese
½ cup castor sugar
2 teaspoons lemon juice
2 egg yolks
1 tablespoon poppy seeds
2 cups plain flour
CREAM CHEESE FILLING
¾ cup dried apricots
40g packaged cream cheese
1 egg white

Beat butter, cream cheese and sugar in small bowl with electric mixer until light and fluffy; beat in juice and egg yolks. Stir in seeds and sifted flour. Mix to a firm dough; cover, refrigerate for 30 minutes.

Divide dough into 4 portions. Roll 1 portion between sheets of greaseproof paper until 3mm thick. Cut into 6cm squares. Spread a level teaspoon of filling over a square, leaving 1 corner un-covered. Roll into crescent shape, starting from the corner covered with filling, press uncovered corner to seal; turn ends in. Repeat with remaining filling and dough.

Place crescents about 2cm apart on greased oven trays. Bake in moderate oven for about 20 minutes or until lightly browned; cool on wire racks. Dust with sifted icing sugar, if desired.
Cream Cheese Filling: Cover apricots with boiling water, cover, stand for 1 hour; drain. Blend or process apricots, cheese and egg white until smooth.

Makes about 40.

PEANUT CHOCOLATE SLICE

90g butter
¾ cup brown sugar, firmly packed
2 tablespoons honey
2 tablespoons smooth peanut butter
1 cup plain flour
¼ cup self-raising flour
¾ cup rolled oats
¾ cup unsalted roasted peanuts, chopped
CHOCOLATE TOPPING
125g dark chocolate, chopped
90g unsalted butter

Grease 20cm x 30cm lamington pan. Combine butter, sugar, honey and peanut butter in pan, stir over heat until combined. Remove from heat, stir in sifted flours, oats and nuts.

Press mixture into prepared pan. Bake in moderate oven for about 20 minutes or until well browned; cool in pan. Spread cold slice with chocolate topping; refrigerate until set.
Chocolate Topping: Combine chocolate and butter in pan, stir over low heat until melted and smooth.

RIGHT: Clockwise from back: Almond and Redcurrant Kisses, Peanut Chocolate Slice, Poppy Seed and Apricot Crescents.

SPICY DATE AND PECAN COOKIES

180g butter
2 teaspoons vanilla essence
½ cup castor sugar
1 egg yolk
1½ cups self-raising flour
1 teaspoon ground cinnamon
½ teaspoon ground nutmeg
⅔ cup chopped dates
½ cup pecans, chopped
⅔ cup pecan halves

Beat butter, essence, sugar and egg yolk in small bowl with electric mixer until light and fluffy. Stir in sifted flour and spices, then dates and chopped pecans; refrigerate for 30 minutes.

Roll 2 level teaspoons of mixture into a ball, place on greased oven tray. Repeat with remaining mixture, allowing about 4cm between cookies. Top with pecan halves. Bake in moderately hot oven for about 12 minutes or until lightly browned; cool on trays.

Makes about 50.

ALMOND HONEY BARS

1 cup plain flour
½ teaspoon ground nutmeg
½ cup packaged ground almonds
½ cup brown sugar, firmly packed
90g butter, melted
1½ cups (210g) slivered almonds

TOPPING
3 eggs, lightly beaten
¼ cup brown sugar
¼ cup honey
100g milk chocolate, melted

Grease 20cm x 30cm lamington pan. Combine sifted flour and nutmeg, ground almonds, sugar and butter in bowl. Press mixture evenly over base of prepared pan. Bake in moderate oven for about 12 minutes or until lightly browned; cool.

Pour topping over base, sprinkle with slivered almonds. Bake in moderately slow oven for about 40 minutes or until topping is set. Cool in pan, refrigerate for several hours before cutting.
Topping: Combine eggs, sugar and honey in bowl; stir in chocolate.

NUTTY ROCKY ROAD SLICE

¾ cup plain flour
¼ cup self-raising flour
½ cup walnut pieces
⅓ cup castor sugar
125g butter, melted
¼ cup coconut
TOPPING
150g milk chocolate, melted
90g butter, melted
2 tablespoons water
¼ cup walnut pieces
¼ cup unsalted roasted peanuts
100g packet pink marshmallows, halved
⅓ cup red glace cherries, chopped

Grease 20cm x 30cm lamington pan. Combine sifted flours, walnuts, sugar and butter in bowl. Press mixture evenly over base of prepared pan, bake in moderate oven for about 15 minutes or until lightly browned; cool.

Spread topping over base, sprinkle with coconut; refrigerate until set.
Topping: Combine chocolate and butter in bowl, stir in remaining ingredients.

RIGHT: Clockwise from front: Spicy Date and Pecan Cookies, Nutty Rocky Road Slice, Almond Honey Bars.

China and spoon from Appley Hoare Antiques

PEANUT CREAM CHEESE SPIRALS

2 cups plain flour
⅔ cup icing sugar
60g butter
125g packet cream cheese
1 egg, lightly beaten
icing sugar, extra
CREAMY NUT FILLING
¼ cup crunchy peanut butter
60g packaged cream cheese
1 tablespoon icing sugar
1 tablespoon water

Sift flour and icing sugar into bowl, rub in butter and cream cheese. Stir in egg; mix to a firm dough. Cover, refrigerate dough for 30 minutes.

Roll dough between sheets of greaseproof paper to a rectangle about 25cm x 40cm. Spread evenly with filling. Roll up dough from each long side to meet in centre; cover, refrigerate until firm.

Cut roll into 5mm slices. Place slices on greased oven trays about 2cm apart. Bake in moderate oven for about 20 minutes or until lightly browned. Stand for 5 minutes before lifting onto wire racks to cool. Dust half of each biscuit with sifted extra icing sugar.

Creamy Nut Filling: Beat peanut butter, cheese, sifted icing sugar and water in small bowl with electric mixer until just combined.

Makes about 50.

CHOC-ORANGE HAZELNUT CRESCENTS

125g butter
2 teaspoons grated orange rind
2 tablespoons castor sugar
¾ cup plain flour
½ cup packaged ground hazelnuts
60g dark chocolate, melted

Cream butter, rind and sugar in small bowl with electric mixer until light and fluffy. Stir in sifted flour and hazelnuts. Turn dough onto lightly floured surface, knead until smooth; cover, refrigerate 30 minutes.

Roll 2 level teaspoons of mixture into sausage shape about 7cm long, curve into crescent shape; place onto greased oven tray. Repeat with remaining mixture, allowing about 3cm between crescents. Bake in moderate oven for about 15 minutes or until lightly browned, cool on trays. Transfer crescents onto wire racks, pipe or drizzle with chocolate.

Makes about 25.

MACADAMIA AND WHITE CHOCOLATE COOKIES

125g butter
2 teaspoons vanilla essence
1 cup brown sugar, firmly packed
1 egg
1 cup plain flour
½ cup self-raising flour
1 cup (150g) chopped unsalted roasted macadamia nuts
1 cup (70g) shredded coconut
¾ cup rolled oats
200g white chocolate, chopped

Beat butter, essence, sugar and egg in small bowl with electric mixer until light and fluffy. Transfer mixture to large bowl, stir in sifted flours, nuts, coconut, oats and chocolate.

Shape level tablespoons of mixture into balls, place about 3cm apart on greased oven trays, flatten slightly. Bake in moderately hot oven for about 12 minutes or until lightly browned; cool cookies on trays.

Makes about 40.

LEFT: From top: Choc-Orange Hazelnut Crescents, Peanut Cream Cheese Spirals. RIGHT: Macadamia and White Chocolate Cookies.

Left: Accessories from Home & Garden. Right: Tray and container from The Country Trader; glass and flour bag from Appley Hoare Antiques

STICKY PECAN
AND LEMON SLICE

250g butter
1 teaspoon vanilla essence
1/4 cup castor sugar
2 cups plain flour
1/3 cup pecans, chopped
TOPPING
2 eggs
1 cup castor sugar
1/4 cup rice flour
1 teaspoon grated lemon rind
1/4 cup lemon juice

Grease 20cm x 30cm lamington pan, line
with foil.

Beat butter, essence and sugar in
small bowl with electric mixer until light
and fluffy. Stir in sifted flour and nuts.
Press mixture into prepared pan, bake in
moderate oven for about 20 minutes or
until lightly browned; cool.

Pour topping over base, bake in
moderate oven for about further 20
minutes or until lightly browned. Cool in
pan; stand for several hours or overnight
before cutting.
Topping: Beat eggs in small bowl with
electric mixer until thick and foamy.
Gradually add the sugar, beating well
between each addition (it is not necessary
to dissolve sugar). Stir in flour, rind and
juice.

WALNUT COFFEE CREAMS

1 cup (120g) walnuts, chopped
250g butter
2 tablespoons coffee and chicory
    essence
1/4 cup castor sugar
1 1/2 cups plain flour
COFFEE CREAM
125g packet cream cheese
1/2 cup icing sugar
1 teaspoon dry instant coffee
1 teaspoon hot water

Blend or process walnuts until finely
ground. Beat butter, essence and sugar in
small bowl with electric mixer until light
and fluffy. Stir in walnuts and flour.

Spoon mixture into piping bag fitted
with fluted tube. Pipe 6cm lengths of mixture about 2cm apart onto greased oven
trays. Bake in moderate oven for about 15
minutes or until crisp and lightly browned;
cool on wire racks.

Spoon coffee cream into piping bag
fitted with fluted tube, pipe onto half the
biscuits, top with remaining biscuits.
Coffee Cream: Beat cheese and sifted
icing sugar in small bowl with electric
mixer until light and fluffy. Beat in combined coffee and water.

Makes about 40.

SCORCHED PEANUT COOKIES

125g butter
1/4 cup crunchy peanut butter
3/4 cup brown sugar, firmly packed
1 egg
1 1/2 cups plain flour
1/2 teaspoon bicarbonate of soda
3/4 cup scorched peanuts

Beat butter, peanut butter, sugar and egg
in small bowl with electric mixer until well
combined. Transfer mixture to large bowl,
stir in sifted dry ingredients and nuts. Roll
2 level teaspoons of mixture into a ball
with lightly floured hands. Place onto
greased oven tray, flatten slightly with fork.
Repeat with remaining mixture, allowing
about 3cm between cookies. Bake in
moderately hot oven for about 12 minutes
or until lightly browned; cool on trays.

Makes about 50.

*RIGHT: Clockwise from front: Walnut Coffee
Creams, Sticky Pecan and Lemon Slice,
Scorched Peanut Cookies.*

SHORTBREAD

Luscious, sweet and buttery, shortbread has a rich, crumbly texture usually derived from the rice flour, ground rice, cornflour or custard powder added to butter and flour. For equally good results, rice flour and ground rice can be substituted for each other, although rice flour is finer. However, before attempting any of the following shortbread delights, turn to the back of this book and read through our "Hints For Success" section.

FRUIT MINCE TRIANGLES

2 cups plain flour
¼ cup cornflour
¼ cup custard powder
⅓ cup icing sugar
200g butter, chopped
¼ cup water, approximately
410g jar fruit mince
1½ tablespoons cornflour, extra
1 tablespoon castor sugar

Lightly grease 25cm x 30cm Swiss roll pan. Sift flours, custard powder and icing sugar into bowl. Rub in butter, stir in enough water to mix to a firm dough; cover, refrigerate for 30 minutes.

Cut dough in half, roll half the dough between sheets of greaseproof paper until large enough to line prepared pan, trim edges. Cover pastry with paper, fill with dried beans or rice. Bake in hot oven for 7 minutes, remove paper and beans, bake about further 7 minutes or until lightly browned. Cool slightly, spread base with combined fruit mince and extra cornflour. Roll remaining dough until large enough to cover fruit mince mixture, trim edges.

Mark top layer of pastry into triangles, brush lightly with water. Sprinkle with castor sugar; prick with fork. Bake in hot oven for about 20 minutes or until lightly browned. Cool in pan before cutting.

PECAN SHORTBREADS

250g butter
1 teaspoon vanilla essence
⅓ cup castor sugar
2¼ cups plain flour
¼ cup rice flour
⅓ cup pecans, finely chopped
⅔ cup (100g) Choc Melts, melted
1 cup (100g) pecans, approximately, extra

Beat butter, essence and sugar in small bowl with electric mixer until light and fluffy. Transfer to large bowl. Stir in sifted flours and chopped nuts, mix to a soft dough. Turn dough onto lightly floured surface, knead until smooth; cover, refrigerate for 30 minutes.

Roll dough between sheets of greaseproof paper until 6mm thick. Cut 8cm diamonds from dough, place about 3cm apart on greased oven trays. Bake in moderately slow oven for about 20 minutes or until lightly browned. Stand few minutes before lifting onto wire racks to cool. Secure extra nuts to each biscuit with Choc Melts; pipe remaining Choc Melts over biscuits.

Makes about 50.

LEFT: Fruit Mince Triangles.
RIGHT: Pecan Shortbreads.

GLAZED LEMON SHORTBREADS

2 tablespoons rice flour
⅓ cup icing sugar
2 cups plain flour
250g butter
1 teaspoon grated lemon rind
2 teaspoons lemon juice,
   approximately
LEMON GLAZE
1 cup icing sugar
½ teaspoon grated lemon rind
¼ cup lemon juice

Lightly grease 20cm x 30cm lamington pan. Sift dry ingredients into bowl, rub in butter, stir in rind and enough juice to make ingredients cling together. Turn dough onto lightly floured surface, knead lightly until smooth. Press dough evenly into prepared pan, mark into finger lengths. Bake in moderately slow oven for about 40 minutes or until lightly browned.

Cut into finger lengths in pan, stand for 10 minutes, lift onto wire rack to cool. Dip an end of each biscuit in glaze, place on foil-covered tray to set.
Lemon Glaze: Combine sifted icing sugar, rind and juice in bowl; beat until well combined.

TRADITIONAL SCOTCH SHORTBREAD

250g butter
1 teaspoon vanilla essence
⅓ cup castor sugar
2¼ cups plain flour
¼ cup rice flour

Beat butter, essence and sugar in small bowl with electric mixer until light and fluffy; transfer to large bowl. Stir in sifted flours in 2 batches. Press mixture together firmly. Turn dough onto lightly floured surface, knead for 3 minutes.

Divide mixture in half, roll each half on greased oven tray until 18cm round, push into shape, pinch edges. Mark 8 wedges on surface of each round, prick with fork. Bake in moderately slow oven for about 1¼ hours or until lightly browned. Cool before breaking into wedges.

CHOCOLATE CHIP SHORTBREAD MUSHROOMS

250g butter
1 teaspoon vanilla essence
⅓ cup castor sugar
2 cups plain flour
¾ cup cornflour
¾ cup (140g) Choc Bits

Beat butter, essence and sugar in small bowl with electric mixer until light and fluffy; transfer to large bowl. Stir in sifted flours and Choc Bits. Turn dough onto lightly floured surface, knead lightly until smooth; cover, refrigerate for 30 minutes.

Roll dough between sheets of greaseproof paper until 7mm thick, cut 7cm mushroom shapes from dough, place about 3cm apart onto greased oven trays. Bake in moderately hot oven for about 10 minutes or until lightly browned. Stand for 3 minutes before lifting onto wire racks to cool.

Makes about 60.

RIGHT: From back: Chocolate Chip Shortbread Mushrooms, Traditional Scotch Shortbread, Glazed Lemon Shortbreads.

PISTACHIO LEMON CUSHIONS

125g butter
2 teaspoons grated lemon rind
⅓ cup castor sugar
1 cup self-raising flour
¼ cup plain flour
¼ cup cornflour
3 teaspoons lemon juice
1 egg white, lightly beaten
1 tablespoon coffee crystals
CREAM CHEESE FILLING
60g packaged cream cheese
2 tablespoons lemon butter
⅓ cup chopped pistachio nuts

Beat butter, rind and sugar in small bowl with electric mixer until light and fluffy. Stir in sifted flours with juice, mix to a firm dough. Turn dough onto lightly floured surface, knead gently until smooth; cover, refrigerate for 30 minutes.

Roll dough between sheets of greaseproof paper until 4mm thick. Cut 4cm rounds from dough, place half the rounds about 3cm apart on greased oven trays. Place ½ level teaspoon of filling onto centre of each round on trays; brush edges with egg white. Top with remaining rounds, press edges together. Brush tops with a little more egg white, sprinkle with coffee crystals. Bake in moderately hot oven for about 10 minutes or until lightly browned; cool on trays.

Cream Cheese Filling: Beat cheese and lemon butter in small bowl until smooth, stir in nuts.

Makes about 40.

SOUR CREAM AND LEMON SHORTBREADS

125g butter
2 teaspoons grated lemon rind
¾ cup icing sugar
1½ cups plain flour
¼ cup sour cream
1 tablespoon lemon juice
¼ cup mixed peel, approximately
icing sugar, extra

Beat butter, rind and sifted icing sugar in small bowl with electric mixer until creamy. Stir in sifted flour, cream and juice.

Spoon mixture into piping bag fitted with 1cm star tube. Pipe 2cm rosettes of mixture about 3cm apart onto greased oven trays; top with a little mixed peel. Bake in moderately hot oven for about 8 minutes or until lightly browned. Stand for 5 minutes before lifting onto wire racks to cool. Dust with sifted extra icing sugar.

Makes about 75.

LEFT: From back: Pistachio Lemon Cushions, Sour Cream and Lemon Shortbreads.

GREEK SHORTBREAD

250g unsalted butter
1 teaspoon vanilla essence
1 cup castor sugar
1 egg
¼ cup brandy
¾ cup blanched almonds, toasted,
finely chopped
1½ cups self-raising flour
2½ cups plain flour
½ teaspoon ground nutmeg
¼ cup rose flower water
½ cup water
3 cups icing sugar

Beat butter, essence and sugar in small bowl with electric mixer until light and fluffy. Beat in egg and brandy, transfer mixture to large bowl. Stir in almonds and sifted dry ingredients in 2 batches.

Turn dough onto floured surface, knead gently until smooth. Shape level tablespoons of dough into crescent shapes, place about 3cm apart onto greased oven trays. Bake in moderate oven for about 15 minutes or until lightly browned.

Lift shortbread onto wire racks, brush hot shortbread with combined rose flower water and water, cover with sifted icing sugar; cool.

Makes about 50.

VANILLA CREAM SHORTBREADS

180g butter
1 teaspoon vanilla essence
⅓ cup icing sugar
1 cup self-raising flour
½ cup plain flour
½ cup custard powder
CREAM FILLING
50g butter
1 teaspoon vanilla essence
1 tablespoon sweetened
condensed milk
½ cup icing sugar

Beat butter, essence and sifted icing sugar in small bowl with electric mixer until smooth. Stir in sifted dry ingredients.

Roll 2 level teaspoons of mixture into a ball, place onto greased oven tray, press lightly with fork. Repeat with remaining mixture, allowing about 5cm between biscuits. Bake in moderately hot oven for about 12 minutes or until lightly browned; cool on trays. Join shortbread biscuits with cream filling.

Cream Filling: Beat butter, essence and condensed milk in bowl until combined, gradually beat in sifted icing sugar.

Makes about 20.

BUTTERSCOTCH SHORTBREAD ROSETTES

250g butter
1 teaspoon vanilla essence
½ cup brown sugar, firmly packed
2 cups plain flour

Beat butter, essence and sugar in small bowl with electric mixer until light and fluffy, stir in sifted flour, mix to a soft dough.

Spoon mixture into piping bag fitted with star tube, pipe rosettes about 3cm apart onto greased oven trays. Bake in moderate oven for about 12 minutes or until lightly browned; cool on trays.

Makes about 35.

ABOVE: Greek Shortbread.
RIGHT: From front: Vanilla Cream Shortbreads, Butterscotch Shortbread Rosettes.

Right: China from Corso de Fiori

CHOCOLATE-DIPPED MOCHA SHORTBREAD

2 cups plain flour
2 tablespoons rice flour
⅓ cup icing sugar
250g butter, chopped
1⅔ cups (250g) Milk Melts, melted
COFFEE LAYER
1 teaspoon dry instant coffee
1 teaspoon hot water
2 tablespoons icing sugar
1 tablespoon plain flour
CHOCOLATE LAYER
¼ cup icing sugar
2 tablespoons cocoa
2 teaspoons chocolate topping

Line 8cm x 26cm bar pan with foil. Sift flours and icing sugar into bowl, rub in butter, press mixture firmly together (or process ingredients until mixture forms a ball). Turn dough onto lightly floured surface, knead until smooth.

Divide dough evenly into 3 portions. Press 1 portion evenly over base of prepared pan. Press coffee layer evenly over plain layer, then top with chocolate layer; cover, refrigerate for 30 minutes.

Remove shortbread from pan, peel away foil. Cut shortbread into thin slices, place about 3cm apart onto greased oven trays. Bake in moderate oven for about 20 minutes or until lightly coloured. Cool shortbread on trays.

Dip shortbread into Milk Melts, place on foil-covered trays, stand until set.

Coffee Layer: Dissolve coffee in hot water; cool. Knead coffee mixture into 1 portion of dough with sifted icing sugar and flour; knead until smooth.

Chocolate Layer: Knead sifted icing sugar and cocoa into remaining portion of dough with chocolate topping. Knead dough until smooth.

Makes about 50.

HAZELNUT BOWS

125g butter
1 teaspoon vanilla essence
¼ cup castor sugar
1 egg yolk
1 cup plain flour
2 tablespoons self-raising flour
¼ cup cornflour
½ cup packaged ground hazelnuts

Beat butter, essence, sugar and egg yolk in small bowl with electric mixer until light and fluffy. Stir in sifted flours and nuts. Turn onto floured surface, knead until smooth; cover, refrigerate 30 minutes.

Roll dough between sheets of greaseproof paper until 5mm thick. Cut 3cm x 6cm rectangles from dough, place about 3cm apart on greased oven trays; pinch centres together. Bake in moderate oven for about 15 minutes or until lightly browned; cool on trays. Dust with sifted icing sugar, if desired.

Makes about 40.

PLUM JAM AND ALMOND DROPS

1½ cups plain flour
1½ tablespoons rice flour
¼ cup icing sugar
**2 tablespoons packaged ground
    almonds**
¼ teaspoon almond essence
180g butter, chopped
⅓ cup plum jam, warmed
¼ cup flaked almonds

Sift flours and icing sugar into bowl, stir in ground almonds and essence, rub in butter. Press mixture firmly together (or process ingredients until mixture forms a ball). Turn dough onto lightly floured surface, knead gently until smooth.

Roll 2 level teaspoons of dough into a ball, place onto greased oven tray. Indent biscuit, using handle of wooden spoon, fill cavity with a little jam, top with a flaked almond. Repeat with remaining dough, jam and almonds, allowing about 4cm between biscuits. Bake in moderate oven for about 20 minutes or until lightly browned; cool on trays.

Makes about 35.

RASPBERRY SHORTBREAD HEARTS

2 tablespoons rice flour
2 tablespoons icing sugar
2 tablespoons cornflour
1 cup plain flour
125g unsalted butter
85g packet raspberry jelly crystals
2 teaspoons water, approximately
2 tablespoons raspberry jam
1 cup (150g) White Melts, melted
3 teaspoons oil

Sift dry ingredients into large bowl, rub in butter, stir in jelly crystals. Add enough water to make ingredients cling together; cover, refrigerate for 30 minutes.

Roll dough between sheets of greaseproof paper until 3mm thick. Cut out 5cm shapes, place about 3cm apart onto greased oven trays. Bake in moderately slow oven for about 25 minutes or until firm to touch, but not browned. Stand for 5 minutes before lifting onto wire racks to cool.

Sandwich hearts with jam, dip into combined White Melts and oil, place onto foil-covered trays; stand until set.

Makes about 25.

ABOVE: Raspberry Shortbread Hearts.
LEFT: Clockwise from front:
Chocolate-Dipped Mocha Shortbread,
Hazelnut Bows, Plum Jam and Almond Drops.

Above: China from Mikasa

MERINGUES AND MACAROONS

The great thing about meringues and macaroons is that you get heaps for your money, and they will be perfect every time if you make sure the sugar is dissolved in the egg white before cooking. When cooked correctly, and without filling, meringues and macaroons will keep in an airtight container for weeks, ready to dress up when you want an especially glamorous treat. They're also great used as the base or topping for quick and easy desserts. So never throw away an egg white; whisk it to bliss!

CINNAMON ALMOND STARS

2 egg whites
3¼ cups (520g) pure icing sugar
2 cups (240g) packaged ground almonds
1 tablespoon ground cinnamon
pure icing sugar, extra

Beat egg whites in small bowl with wooden spoon until frothy, gradually beat in sifted icing sugar. Reserve ½ cup of mixture for topping; cover to keep airtight.

Stir almonds and cinnamon into remaining icing sugar mixture. Turn paste onto surface dusted with extra sifted icing sugar, knead until smooth. Roll paste out until 5mm thick. Spread top evenly with reserved icing sugar mixture. Stand, uncovered, for about 30 minutes or until topping is dry to touch.

Cut paste into 3½cm shapes, place about 2cm apart onto greased oven trays. Bake in very slow oven for about 20 minutes or until topping is set, but not browned. Stand on tray for 5 minutes before lifting onto wire racks to cool.

Makes about 25.

CARROT CONFETTI MERINGUES

¼ cup finely grated carrot
2 egg whites
⅔ cup castor sugar
1 teaspoon lemon juice
⅔ cup (100g) Choc Melts, melted

Chop grated carrot finely. Beat egg whites in small bowl with electric mixer until soft peaks form. Gradually add sugar and juice; beat until dissolved between each addition. Squeeze excess liquid from carrot, stir into meringue mixture.

Spoon mixture into piping bag fitted with 1½cm star tube. Pipe 3cm rosettes about 4cm apart onto foil-covered oven trays. Bake in slow oven for about 45 minutes or until firm; turn oven off, cool meringue in oven. Dip half of each meringue into Choc Melts, place onto foil-covered trays until set.

Makes about 70.

LEFT: Cinnamon Almond Stars.
ABOVE: Carrot Confetti Meringues.

CORN FLAKE COCONUT MACAROONS

4 egg whites
1½ cups castor sugar
1 teaspoon vanilla essence
½ cup crushed nuts
½ cup shredded coconut
3 cups (90g) Corn Flakes, lightly crushed
½ cup plain flour

Beat egg whites in small bowl with electric mixer until soft peaks form, gradually add sugar, beat until dissolved between each addition. Transfer mixture to large bowl, fold in essence, nuts, coconut, Corn Flakes and sifted flour in 2 batches.

Place level tablespoons of mixture about 4cm apart on greased oven trays. Bake in moderately slow oven for about 30 minutes or until lightly browned and crisp. Cool on trays.

Makes about 50.

COFFEE MERINGUE TWISTS

1 egg white
⅓ cup castor sugar
1 teaspoon dry instant coffee
1 teaspoon hot water

Beat egg white in small bowl with electric mixer until soft peaks form, gradually add sugar, beat until dissolved between additions. Stir in combined coffee and water.

Spoon mixture into piping bag fitted with small fluted tube, pipe mixture into twists about 5cm apart on foil-covered oven trays. Bake in very slow oven for about 1 hour or until meringues are firm to touch. Turn oven off, allow meringues to cool in oven.

Makes about 35.

ABOVE: From top: Coffee Meringue Twists, Corn Flake Coconut Macaroons.
RIGHT: Mini Meringue Pearl Shells.

MINI MERINGUE PEARL SHELLS

2 egg whites
½ cup castor sugar
1 teaspoon grated orange rind
apricot food colouring
¼ cup thickened cream
silver cachous

Beat egg whites in small bowl with electric mixer until soft peaks form; gradually add sugar, beat until dissolved between each addition. Beat in rind, tint with colouring.

Spoon mixture into piping bag fitted with 1½cm star tube. Pipe small shell shapes onto foil-covered trays. Bake in very slow oven for about 1 hour or until meringues are dry to touch. Turn oven off, cool meringues in oven.

Whip cream until firm peaks form, use to join meringues like an open shell. Use cachous to represent pearls.

Makes about 50.

CHOCOLATE HAZELNUT MERINGUES

4 egg whites
1¼ cups castor sugar
1 teaspoon lemon juice
FILLING
⅔ cup chocolate hazelnut spread
¼ cup roasted hazelnuts, finely
chopped

Beat egg whites in small bowl with electric mixer until soft peaks form. Gradually add sugar, beat until dissolved between each addition; beat in juice.

Spoon mixture into piping bag fitted with 1cm star tube, pipe 2cm x 5cm shapes about 3cm apart on foil-covered oven trays. Bake in very slow oven for about 40 minutes or until firm and dry; cool on trays. Sandwich meringues with filling.
Filling: Combine spread and nuts in bowl.
Makes about 35.

CHOCOLATE APRICOT MACAROONS

¾ cup finely chopped dried apricots
1 tablespoon Grand Marnier
3 egg whites
¾ cup castor sugar
1¾ cups (160g) coconut
⅓ cup (50g) White Melts, melted
⅓ cup (50g) White Melts, melted,
extra
⅓ cup (50g) Choc Melts, melted

Combine apricots and liqueur in bowl; stand for 15 minutes.

Beat egg whites in small bowl with electric mixer until soft peaks form, gradually add sugar, beat until dissolved between each addition. Fold in apricot mixture, coconut and White Melts.

Spoon mixture into piping bag fitted with 2cm plain tube. Pipe 4cm lengths of mixture about 4cm apart on foil-covered oven trays. Bake in slow oven for about 25 minutes or until firm. Cool on trays. Lift macaroons onto wire racks; drizzle with extra White Melts and Choc Melts.
Makes about 60.

CHOCOLATE CHIP MACAROONS

3 egg whites
¾ cup castor sugar
3 cups (270g) coconut
1 cup (190g) Choc Bits

Beat egg whites in small bowl with electric mixer until soft peaks form, gradually add sugar, beat until dissolved between each addition. Transfer mixture to large bowl, fold in remaining ingredients in 2 batches.

Using wet hands, roll 1 level tablespoon of mixture into a ball, place onto greased oven tray. Repeat with remaining mixture, allowing about 3cm between macaroons. Bake in moderate oven for about 20 minutes or until lightly coloured. Cool on trays.
Makes about 40.

RIGHT: Clockwise from bottom: Chocolate Chip Macaroons, Chocolate Apricot Macaroons, Chocolate Hazelnut Macaroons.

China from Royal Doulton

MERINGUE KISSES WITH STRAWBERRY CREAM

2 egg whites
⅔ cup castor sugar
1 teaspoon lemon juice
STRAWBERRY CREAM
60g butter
¼ teaspoon strawberry essence
1 cup icing sugar
pink food colouring

Beat egg whites in small bowl with electric mixer until soft peaks form. Gradually add sugar and juice, beat until dissolved between each addition.

Spoon mixture into piping bag fitted with 1½cm star tube. Pipe 2cm rosettes of mixture about 2cm apart onto foil-covered oven trays. Bake in very slow oven for about 45 minutes or until firm. Turn oven off, cool meringues in oven.

Sandwich cold meringues with strawberry cream.

Strawberry Cream: Beat butter and essence in small bowl with electric mixer until light and fluffy. Gradually beat in sifted icing sugar. Tint pale pink with colouring.

Makes about 40.

APRICOT ALMOND MACAROONS

½ cup finely chopped
 dried apricots
2 egg whites
½ cup castor sugar
2 cups (180g) coconut
½ cup slivered almonds
1 teaspoon grated lemon rind

Place apricots in bowl, cover with boiling water, stand for 1 hour; drain.

Beat egg whites in small bowl with electric mixer until soft peaks form, gradually add sugar, beat until dissolved between each addition. Stir in apricots, coconut, almonds and rind.

Place level tablespoons of mixture onto greased oven trays, allowing about 4cm between macaroons. Bake in moderate oven for about 20 minutes or until lightly browned. Loosen macaroons, cool on trays.

Makes about 30.

CHERRY PINK MACAROONS

3 cups (270g) coconut
400g can sweetened condensed milk
1 cup (210g) red glace cherries, finely
 chopped
1 cup (90g) coconut, extra
½ cup red glace cherries, quartered,
 extra

Combine coconut, condensed milk and cherries in bowl; mix well. Shape 2 level teaspoons of mixture into a ball, toss in extra coconut, place onto greased oven tray; decorate with a cherry quarter. Repeat with remaining mixture and extra cherries, allowing about 3cm between macaroons. Bake in moderate oven for about 15 minutes or until lightly browned.

Stand on tray for 2 minutes before lifting onto wire racks to cool.

Makes about 60.

LEFT: Top row from left: Apricot Almond Macaroons, Cherry Pink Macaroons.
ABOVE: Meringue Kisses with Strawberry Cream.

Left: Jars from Appley Hoare Antiques

ALMOND LIQUEUR MACAROONS

2 egg whites
¾ cup castor sugar
1 tablespoon Amaretto
2 cups (240g) packaged ground almonds
1 cup (80g) flaked almonds, lightly crushed

Beat egg whites in small bowl with electric mixer until soft peaks form. Gradually add sugar, beat until dissolved between each addition. Stir in liqueur and ground and flaked almonds.

Drop level tablespoons of mixture onto greased oven trays, allowing about 3cm between macaroons. Bake in moderate oven for about 20 minutes or until lightly browned. Cool macaroons on trays.

Makes about 35.

CINNAMON HAZELNUT MERINGUES

3 egg whites
¾ cup castor sugar
½ cup packaged ground hazelnuts
1 teaspoon ground cinnamon
1⅔ cups (250g) Milk Melts, melted
1 teaspoon oil

Cover oven trays with baking paper, mark 5cm circles on paper about 3cm apart.

Beat egg whites in small bowl with electric mixer until soft peaks form. Gradually beat in sugar, beat until dissolved between each addition. Fold in nuts and cinnamon.

Spoon mixture into piping bag fitted with 5mm plain tube. Pipe mixture in marked circles, smooth tops. Bake in very slow oven for about 45 minutes or until dry to touch. Turn oven off, cool in oven.

Dip edge of meringues in combined Milk Melts and oil, stand on foil-covered trays. Drizzle remaining chocolate over meringues, stand until set.

Makes about 60.

CHOCOLATE PISTACHIO MACAROONS

2 egg whites
½ cup castor sugar
1 teaspoon vanilla essence
1 cup (90g) coconut
½ cup chopped pistachio nuts
200g milk chocolate, melted
¼ cup chopped pistachio nuts, extra

Beat egg whites in small bowl with electric mixer until soft peaks form, gradually add sugar, beat until dissolved between additions. Stir in essence, coconut and nuts.

Drop 2 level teaspoons of mixture together onto foil-covered tray. Repeat with remaining mixture, allowing about 3cm between macaroons. Bake in moderate oven for about 15 minutes or until lightly browned. Cool on trays.

Dip top of each macaroon in chocolate, sprinkle with extra nuts.

Makes about 45.

RIGHT: Clockwise from front: Chocolate Pistachio Macaroons, Cinnamon Hazelnut Meringues, Almond Liqueur Macaroons.

FRUIT

Fruit is very easy to cook with as it readily yields distinctive flavours and colours, and blends healthfully with many other ingredients. We have used all the most popular varieties of fresh and dried fruits, in treats ranging from smart little dainties and scrumptious slices to satisfying lunchbox fillers. First, though, turn to our "Hints for Success" at the back of this book.

DATE AND LEMON SLICE

125g butter
2 teaspoons grated lemon rind
½ cup castor sugar
1 egg
2¼ cups plain flour
1 tablespoon castor sugar, extra
FILLING
1 cup (160g) chopped dates
¾ cup water
2 tablespoons castor sugar
¼ teaspoon ground cinnamon
¼ teaspoon ground nutmeg

Grease 20cm x 30cm lamington pan. Beat butter, rind, sugar and egg in bowl with electric mixer until light and fluffy. Stir in sifted flour, mix to a soft dough. Turn dough onto lightly floured surface, knead gently until smooth; cover, refrigerate for 30 minutes.

Cut dough in half, roll out 1 half between sheets of greaseproof paper until large enough to cover base of prepared pan. Bake in moderately hot oven for about 10 minutes or until lightly browned; cool for 5 minutes.

Spread cold filling evenly over base. Roll out remaining dough until large enough to cover filling, brush lightly with water, sprinkle with extra sugar. Bake in moderately hot oven for about 25 minutes or until lightly browned.
Filling: Combine dates and water in pan, bring to boil, simmer, uncovered, for about 5 minutes or until mixture is thick. Remove from heat, stir in sugar and spices; cool.

BANANA CHIP COOKIES

125g butter
1 teaspoon vanilla essence
½ cup castor sugar
1 egg
1⅓ cups self-raising flour
½ cup (40g) banana chips, chopped
½ cup chopped pecans or walnuts
½ cup (40g) banana chips, extra

Beat butter, essence, sugar and egg in bowl with electric mixer until just combined. Stir in sifted flour, chopped banana chips and nuts.

Shape 2 level teaspoons of mixture into a ball, place onto greased oven tray, top with an extra banana chip. Repeat with remaining mixture and banana chips, leaving about 5cm between cookies. Bake in moderately hot oven for about 12 minutes or until lightly browned. Cool cookies on trays.

Makes about 50.

RIGHT: From back: Date and Lemon Slice, Banana Chip Cookies.

Bowl from Corso de Fiori; bottle from Accoutrement

GLACE FRUIT AND PISTACHIO SLICES

3 egg whites
½ cup castor sugar
1 cup plain flour
½ cup pistachio nuts
¼ cup blanched almonds
2 tablespoons chopped glace
**   pineapple**
2 tablespoons chopped glace apricots
2 tablespoons chopped glace ginger
¼ cup red glace cherries
¼ cup green glace cherries

Grease 8cm x 26cm bar pan, cover base with paper, grease paper. Beat egg whites in small bowl with electric mixer until soft peaks form, gradually add sugar, beat until dissolved between each addition. Stir in sifted flour and remaining ingredients.

Spread mixture into prepared pan, press down firmly. Bake in moderate oven for about 40 minutes or until lightly browned. Stand in pan for 15 minutes before turning onto wire rack to cool.

Wrap bar in foil, stand for 1 to 2 days. Using sharp knife, cut bar into 5mm slices. Place slices onto greased oven trays in single layer. Bake in moderate oven for about 15 minutes or until lightly browned. Cool on trays.

Makes about 55.

BELOW: From back: Vanilla Currant Cookies, Glace Fruit and Pistachio Slices.
RIGHT: Apricot Almond Delights.

Right: Napkin and biscuit barrel from Accoutrement; tile in background from Corso de Fiori. Below: Plates from The Country Trader

VANILLA CURRANT COOKIES

125g butter
1 teaspoon vanilla essence
¾ cup castor sugar
1 egg
2 cups self-raising flour
½ cup coconut
¼ cup currants
VANILLA ICING
1½ cups icing sugar
2 teaspoons vanilla essence
1½ teaspoons soft butter
1½ tablespoons milk, approximately

Beat butter, essence, sugar and egg in small bowl with electric mixer until light and fluffy. Transfer mixture to large bowl, stir in sifted flour, coconut and currants.

Shape 2 level teaspoons of mixture into a ball, place onto greased oven tray; flatten with hand until about 5mm thick. Repeat with remaining mixture, allowing about 5cm between cookies. Bake in moderately hot oven for about 10 minutes or until lightly browned. Cool on trays. Spread cookies thinly with icing, place on wire racks to set.
Vanilla Icing: Sift icing sugar into heatproof bowl, stir in essence and butter, then enough milk to give a thick paste. Stir over hot water until spreadable.

Makes about 40.

APRICOT ALMOND DELIGHTS

1⅔ cups plain flour
⅓ cup packaged ground almonds
⅓ cup castor sugar
125g butter
2 tablespoons water, approximately
icing sugar
FILLING
⅓ cup chopped dried apricots
¼ cup water
1½ tablespoons castor sugar

Sift flour into large bowl, stir in almonds and sugar, rub in butter. Stir in enough water to make ingredients cling together. Turn onto lightly floured surface, knead gently until smooth; cover, refrigerate for 30 minutes.

Roll dough between sheets of greaseproof paper until 4mm thick. Cut equal numbers of 4cm and 5cm rounds from dough. Place level ½ teaspoon of filling in centre of each 4cm round, top with 5cm rounds, press edges together. Place biscuits about 2cm apart onto greased oven trays. Bake in moderately hot oven for about 20 minutes or until lightly browned. Cool on trays. Dust with sifted icing sugar.
Filling: Combine apricots and water in pan, bring to boil, simmer, uncovered, for about 5 minutes or until mixture is thick. Remove from heat, stir in sugar.

Makes about 30.

APRICOT AND APPLE SLICE

1 cup plain flour
⅓ cup castor sugar
90g butter, melted

FILLING
1 cup (160g) finely chopped dried
    apricots
1 cup (90g) finely chopped dried
    apples
1 cup water
¼ cup sugar
2 teaspoons grated lemon rind

TOPPING
2 eggs
¼ cup brown sugar
⅓ cup self-raising flour

Grease 20cm x 30cm lamington pan. Sift flour into bowl, stir in sugar and butter, press mixture firmly over base of prepared pan. Bake in moderate oven for about 20 minutes or until lightly browned; cool.

Spread cold filling over base, then spread with topping. Bake in moderate oven for about 30 minutes or until well browned. Cool in pan before cutting.

Filling: Combine apricots, apples and water in pan, bring to boil, simmer, uncovered for about 10 minutes or until mixture is thick. Remove from heat, stir in sugar and rind; cool to room temperature.

Topping: Beat eggs and sugar in small bowl with electric mixer until thick and creamy. Stir in sifted flour.

CITRUS GINGER BROWNIES

125g unsalted butter, melted
180g dark chocolate, melted
1 cup castor sugar
2 teaspoons grated orange rind
1 tablespoon orange juice
2 eggs
1 cup plain flour
⅓ cup chopped glace ginger
⅓ cup chopped mixed peel
icing sugar

Grease deep 19cm square cake pan, line base with paper, grease paper. Combine butter and chocolate in bowl, stir in sugar, rind and juice. Stir in eggs 1 at a time, then sifted flour, ginger and peel.

Pour mixture into prepared pan. Bake in moderate oven for about 45 minutes or until firm. Cool in pan. Dust with sifted icing sugar before cutting.

CHOCOLATE GINGER ROUNDETTES

75g butter
¼ cup castor sugar
1 egg yolk
1 cup plain flour
½ teaspoon ground ginger
3 teaspoons cocoa
¼ cup glace ginger, finely chopped
1⅓ cups (200g) Choc Melts
1 teaspoon oil

Beat butter, sugar and egg in small bowl with electric mixer until light and fluffy. Stir in sifted dry ingredients and glace ginger. Turn dough onto lightly floured surface, knead until combined; cover, refrigerate for 30 minutes.

Roll dough on lightly floured surface until 4mm thick. Cut 5cm rounds from dough, place onto greased oven trays about 4cm apart. Bake in moderately hot oven for about 10 minutes or until lightly browned. Cool on trays.

Dip half of each biscuit in combined Choc Melts and oil, stand on greaseproof paper until set.

Makes about 30.

SPICY FRUIT MINCE ROLLS

1⅓ cups plain flour
¼ teaspoon ground cinnamon
¼ teaspoon mixed spice
90g butter
1 teaspoon grated lemon rind
1 tablespoon lemon juice
2 tablespoons water, approximately
410g jar (1⅓ cups) fruit mince
⅓ cup rice flour
2 tablespoons castor sugar
¼ teaspoon ground cinnamon, extra

Sift flour and spices into large bowl; rub in butter, stir in rind. Add juice and enough water to make ingredients cling together. Turn onto lightly floured surface, knead gently until smooth; cover, refrigerate for 30 minutes.

Roll dough on lightly floured surface until 2mm thick. Cut 5½cm rounds from dough; roll each round to an oval about 8cm long. Drop 1 level teaspoon of combined fruit mince and rice flour onto centre of each oval. Lightly brush 1 end of each oval with water, roll up. Lightly brush seam side of each roll with water, roll in combined sugar and extra cinnamon.

Place rolls about 3cm apart onto greased oven trays, bake in moderate oven for about 20 minutes or until lightly browned. Cool on trays.

Makes about 40.

LEFT: From left: Citrus Ginger Brownies, Apricot and Apple Slice.
ABOVE: From back: Chocolate Ginger Roundettes, Spicy Fruit Mince Rolls.

APPLE AND CHEESE SLICE

200g butter
½ cup castor sugar
1¼ cups (160g) grated processed
cheddar cheese
1 cup self-raising flour
½ cup plain flour
1 teaspoon ground cinnamon
⅓ cup coconut
¼ cup roasted hazelnuts, chopped
½ cup apple jelly
½ cup finely chopped dried apple

Lightly grease 23cm square slab pan,
cover base with paper, grease paper. Beat
butter and sugar in small bowl with electric
mixer until light and fluffy. Stir in cheese,
sifted flours and cinnamon with coconut.
Mixture will be crumbly at this stage.

Combine half the mixture with hazelnuts, press firmly together; cover, freeze
for about 30 minutes.

Press remaining mixture evenly over
base of prepared pan. Bake in moderate
oven for about 15 minutes or until lightly
browned. Spread with combined apple
jelly and dried apple.

Coarsely grate frozen hazelnut dough
evenly over jelly mixture, press down
lightly. Bake in moderate oven for about
25 minutes or until well browned. Cool in
pan before cutting.

TROPICAL FRUIT COOKIES

125g butter
⅓ cup castor sugar
1 egg
1½ cups (210g) Hawaiian fruit mix
1 cup white self-raising flour
½ cup wholemeal plain flour
ICING
1 cup icing sugar
½ teaspoon coconut essence
1½ tablespoons milk, approximately
1 slice dried pineapple, finely
chopped

Beat butter, sugar and egg in small bowl
with electric mixer until light and fluffy. Stir
in fruit mix and sifted flours.

Roll 1 level tablespoon of mixture into
a ball, place on greased oven tray. Repeat
with remaining mixture, allowing about
5cm between cookies. Bake cookies in
moderately hot oven for about 12 minutes
or until lightly browned. Cool on trays.
Spread cold cookies with icing, stand on
wire rack until set.
Icing: Sift icing sugar into heatproof bowl,
stir in essence and enough milk to make a
firm paste. Stir over hot water until
spreadable; stir in pineapple.

Makes about 25.

*RIGHT: From left: Tropical Fruit Cookies,
Apple and Cheese Slice.*

MILK CHOCOLATE, RUM AND RAISIN SLICE

1 cup (170g) raisins
2 tablespoons dark rum
1 egg
¾ cup brown sugar, firmly packed
200g milk chocolate, melted
125g butter, melted
1¼ cups plain flour
TOPPING
4 egg yolks
⅓ cup castor sugar
¼ cup cream
2 teaspoons dark rum
60g butter
1 teaspoon cocoa

Lightly grease deep 19cm square cake pan. Combine raisins and rum in bowl, stand for 1 hour.

Beat egg and sugar in bowl with electric mixer until frothy. Combine chocolate and butter in large bowl, stir in egg mixture, sifted flour and raisin mixture; spread into prepared pan. Bake in moderate oven for about 30 minutes or until firm. Cool in pan.

Remove cold slice from pan, spread with topping; cover, refrigerate until firm before cutting.

Topping: Combine egg yolks, sugar, cream and rum in pan. Stir over heat, without boiling, until sugar is dissolved and mixture is thickened slightly; cover, cool custard to room temperature.

Beat butter in small bowl with electric mixer until light and fluffy; beat in sifted cocoa. Gradually beat in cold custard, beat until combined; cover, refrigerate for 10 minutes before using.

ABOVE: From left: Milk Chocolate, Rum and Raisin Slice, No-Bake Marmalade Slice.
RIGHT: Cherry Walnut Slice.

NO-BAKE MARMALADE SLICE

1 cup (130g) toasted muesli
3 cups (90g) Rice Bubbles
¾ cup coconut
¼ cup sunflower seed kernels
125g butter
½ cup marmalade
¼ cup crunchy peanut butter
⅓ cup raw sugar

Grease 20cm x 30cm lamington pan. Combine muesli, Rice Bubbles, coconut and kernels in large bowl.

Combine butter, marmalade, peanut butter and sugar in pan, stir over low heat until butter is melted. Bring to boil, simmer, uncovered, without stirring, for 5 minutes. Stir hot mixture into dry ingredients. Press mixture evenly into prepared pan; refrigerate until firm.

CHERRY WALNUT SLICE

¾ cup plain flour
¼ cup self-raising flour
1 tablespoon castor sugar
90g butter
1 egg, separated
3 teaspoons water, approximately
⅓ cup castor sugar, extra
¾ cup chopped red glace cherries
¾ cup chopped walnuts
¼ cup custard powder
icing sugar

Lightly grease 20cm x 30cm lamington pan, line with foil. Sift flours and sugar into bowl, rub in butter, add egg yolk and enough water to mix to a firm dough (or process until just combined). Press dough evenly over base of prepared pan.

Beat egg white in small bowl with electric mixer until soft peaks form, gradually add extra sugar, beat until dissolved between each addition. Stir in cherries, nuts and sifted custard powder; spread evenly over base. Bake in moderate oven for about 25 minutes or until lightly browned. Cool in pan. Dust with sifted icing sugar before cutting.

MIXED PEEL AND CURRANT COOKIES

125g butter
⅔ cup castor sugar
1 egg
¼ cup mixed peel
½ cup currants
2 cups self-raising flour

Beat butter, sugar and egg in small bowl with electric mixer until light and fluffy. Stir in peel, currants and sifted flour.

Roll 2 level teaspoons of mixture into a ball, place onto greased oven tray; flatten slightly. Repeat with remaining mixture, allowing about 4cm between cookies. Bake in moderate oven for about 15 minutes or until lightly browned. Cool cookies on trays.

Makes about 45.

CHERRY CHOCOLATE COOKIES

125g butter
½ cup castor sugar
⅓ cup brown sugar
1 egg
1¾ cups self-raising flour
¾ cup chopped red glace cherries
½ cup (95g) Choc Bits

Beat butter, sugars and egg in small bowl with electric mixer until light and fluffy. Stir in sifted flour, cherries and Choc Bits. Drop 2 level teaspoons of mixture together onto greased oven tray. Repeat with remaining mixture, allowing about 3cm between cookies. Bake in moderate oven for about 12 minutes or until lightly browned. Cool on trays.

Makes about 55.

TANGY LIME COOKIES

60g butter
2 teaspoons grated lime rind
½ cup castor sugar
1 egg yolk
1¼ cups self-raising flour
1 tablespoon lime juice,
    approximately
ICING
3 teaspoons soft butter
1 cup icing sugar
1 tablespoon lime juice,
    approximately

Beat butter, rind, sugar and egg yolk in small bowl with electric mixer until light and fluffy. Stir in sifted flour and enough juice to make ingredients cling together. Turn dough onto lightly floured surface, knead gently until smooth.

Roll 2 level teaspoons of mixture into a ball, place onto greased oven tray, flatten slightly. Repeat with remaining mixture, allowing about 4cm between cookies. Bake in moderate oven for about 15 minutes or until lightly browned. Cool on trays. Spread cold cookies with icing.

Icing: Combine butter and sifted icing sugar in bowl, stir in enough juice to make smooth and spreadable.

Makes about 25.

RIGHT: Clockwise from front: Mixed Peel and Currant Cookies, Tangy Lime Cookies, Cherry Chocolate Cookies.

PASSIONFRUIT CREAMS

1 cup plain flour
½ cup self-raising flour
2 tablespoons cornflour
2 tablespoons custard powder
⅔ cup icing sugar
90g butter
1 egg yolk
¼ cup passionfruit pulp
PASSIONFRUIT CREAM
¼ cup castor sugar
1 tablespoon water
60g unsalted butter
1 tablespoon passionfruit pulp

Sift dry ingredients into bowl, rub in butter. Add egg yolk and passionfruit pulp, mix to a firm dough. Turn dough onto lightly floured surface, knead lightly until smooth; cover, refrigerate for 30 minutes.

Roll dough between sheets of greaseproof paper until 3mm thick. Cut 4½cm squares from dough. Fold opposite corners of each square into centre, press corners together gently. Place onto greased oven trays, allowing about 3cm between biscuits. Bake in moderate oven for about 15 minutes or until lightly browned. Cool on wire racks.

Spoon passionfruit cream into piping bag fitted with small plain tube, pipe cream onto each biscuit.

Passionfruit Cream: Combine sugar and water in pan, stir over heat until sugar is dissolved. Bring to boil, simmer for 2 minutes; cool.

Beat butter in small bowl with electric mixer until light and fluffy, gradually add cold sugar syrup, beat well between each addition. Stir in passionfruit pulp.

Makes about 75.

PRUNE AND APRICOT COOKIES

125g butter
1 teaspoon vanilla essence
⅔ cup brown sugar, firmly packed
1 egg
1¾ cups plain flour
½ teaspoon bicarbonate of soda
½ cup chopped prunes
½ cup chopped dried apricots
1 cup (190g) Choc Bits
icing sugar

Beat butter, essence, sugar and egg in small bowl with electric mixer until light and fluffy. Stir in sifted flour and soda, prunes, apricots and Choc Bits.

Roll 1 level tablespoon of mixture into a ball, place onto lightly greased oven tray, press lightly with fork dipped in flour.

Repeat with remaining mixture, allowing about 2cm between cookies. Bake in moderate oven for about 15 minutes or until lightly browned. Cool on trays. Sprinkle lightly with sifted icing sugar.

Makes about 30.

BANANA ALMOND SLICE

2 cups (250g) Butternut Cookie
  crumbs
100g butter, melted
45g butter, extra
2 tablespoons castor sugar
1 egg yolk
¼ cup custard powder
¼ cup plain flour
1 tablespoon milk
1 cup sliced banana
⅓ cup slivered almonds

Grease 20cm x 30cm lamington pan, line with baking paper. Combine biscuit crumbs and butter in bowl, press evenly over base of prepared pan, refrigerate 30 minutes or until firm.

Beat extra butter, sugar and egg yolk in small bowl with wooden spoon until smooth. Stir in sifted dry ingredients and milk, then banana. Spread mixture evenly over base, sprinkle with almonds. Bake in moderate oven for about 25 minutes or until firm. Cool in pan before cutting.

ABOVE: Passionfruit Creams.
RIGHT: From left: Banana Almond Slice, Prune and Apricot Cookies.

Above: China from Penelope Sach

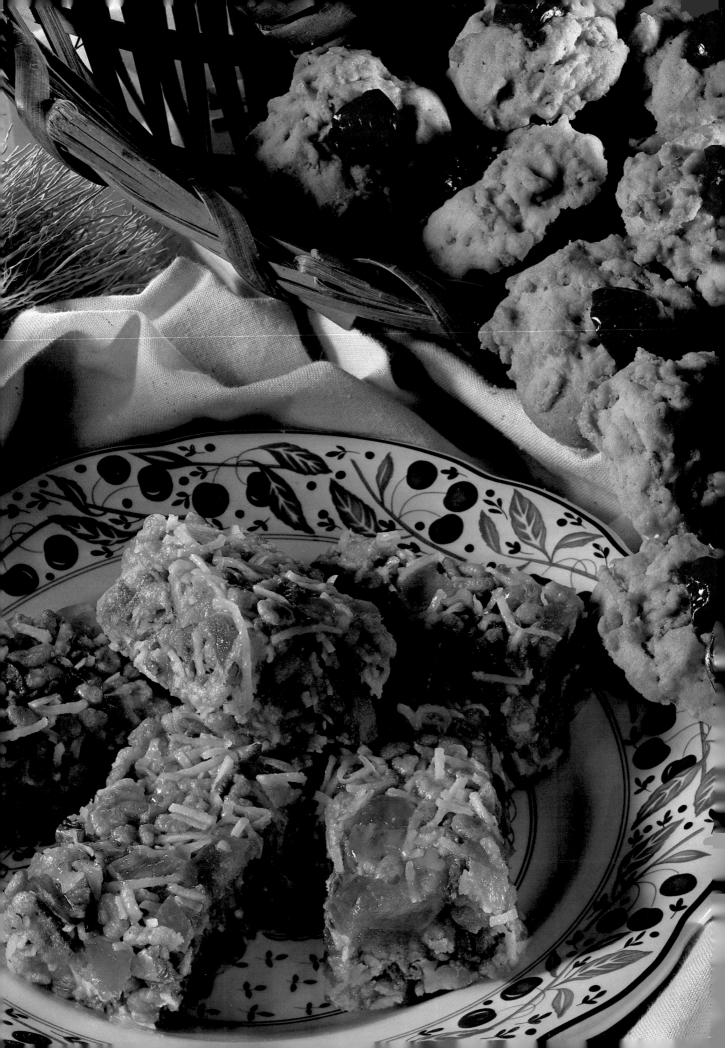

CEREALS

There are many delicious things to chew on in these crunchy biscuits, cookies and slices. Enriched with the natural goodness of cereals, some are smart and many will become nutritious stand-bys for packed lunches. We have used a variety of commercial cereals, plus a variety of brans. A bonus with cereals is that they are a great source of dietary fibre. These recipes are all easy but before beginning, turn to our "Hints for Success" section at the back of this book for general cooking guidelines.

FRUITY COCONUT BUBBLE SLICE

2 cups (140g) shredded coconut
3 cups (90g) Rice Bubbles
⅔ cup All-Bran
1 cup (250g) chopped glace apricots
½ cup chopped glace pineapple
1 cup (125g) chopped pecans or walnuts
125g butter
½ cup coconut cream
½ cup honey
⅓ cup raw sugar

Grease 20cm x 30cm lamington pan. Combine coconut, Rice Bubbles, All-Bran, fruit and nuts in bowl. Combine butter, coconut cream, honey and sugar in pan, stir over low heat, without boiling, until butter is melted and sugar dissolved. Bring to boil, simmer, uncovered, without stirring, for about 5 minutes or until mixture resembles a thick syrup. Stir hot mixture into dry ingredients. Press into prepared pan, refrigerate until firm.

CHERRY OAT COOKIES

125g butter
1 teaspoon vanilla essence
¼ cup brown sugar
1 egg
1 cup self-raising flour
1 cup (80g) Crunchy Oat Bran Cereal
¼ cup red glace cherries, quartered

Beat butter, essence, sugar and egg in small bowl with electric mixer until light and fluffy. Stir in sifted flour and bran, mix to a soft dough.

Drop 2 level teaspoons of mixture together onto greased oven tray, press a cherry quarter onto cookie. Repeat with remaining mixture and cherries, allowing about 5cm between cookies. Bake in moderate oven for about 10 minutes or until lightly browned. Cool few minutes on trays before lifting onto wire racks to cool.

Makes about 40.

LEFT: From back: Cherry Oat Cookies, Fruity Coconut Bubble Slice.

PEANUT BUTTER BUBBLE COOKIES

1½ cups (45g) Rice Bubbles
1 cup plain flour
¼ cup castor sugar
¼ cup unsalted roasted peanuts
¼ cup smooth peanut butter
¼ cup honey
90g butter
1 egg, lightly beaten

Combine Rice Bubbles, sifted flour, sugar and nuts in bowl. Combine peanut butter, honey and butter in pan, stir over low heat until butter is melted. Stir hot mixture into dry ingredients with egg.

Roll level tablespoons of mixture into balls, place about 4cm apart on greased oven trays; flatten slightly. Bake in moderately hot oven for about 10 minutes or until lightly browned; cool on trays.

Makes about 20.

FIG AND GINGER OATIES

1 cup plain flour
1 cup (90g) rolled oats
1 cup (90g) coconut
¾ cup castor sugar
1 cup (190g) chopped dried figs
2 tablespoons chopped glace ginger
125g butter
2 tablespoons golden syrup
2 tablespoons water

Sift flour into bowl, stir in oats, coconut, sugar, figs and ginger. Combine butter, golden syrup and water in pan, stir over low heat until butter is melted. Stir hot butter mixture into flour mixture.

Shape 2 level teaspoons of mixture into a ball, place onto greased oven tray, flatten slightly. Repeat with remaining mixture, allowing about 5cm between cookies. Bake in moderately hot oven for about 12 minutes or until lightly browned; cool on trays.

Makes about 50.

SPICY WHOLEMEAL APRICOT SLICE

90g butter
2 tablespoons castor sugar
⅓ cup brown sugar
1 egg
1 cup (100g) finely crushed Weet-Bix
⅔ cup wholemeal plain flour
⅔ cup white plain flour
1 teaspoon ground ginger
½ teaspoon mixed spice
¼ teaspoon bicarbonate of soda
1 egg white, lightly beaten
2 tablespoons castor sugar, extra
FILLING
1½ cups (240g) chopped dried
    apricots
¾ cup water
2 tablespoons castor sugar

Lightly grease 20cm x 30cm lamington pan. Beat butter, sugars and egg in small bowl with electric mixer until light and fluffy. Stir in Weet-Bix and sifted dry ingredients; mix to a firm dough. Knead dough on lightly floured surface until smooth; cover, refrigerate for 30 minutes.

Roll out half the dough between sheets of greaseproof paper until large enough to cover base of prepared pan. Spread cold filling over base. Roll out remaining pastry large enough to cover filling. Brush lightly with egg white, sprinkle with extra sugar. Bake in moderately hot oven for about 20 minutes or until well browned. Cool in pan before cutting.

Filling: Combine all ingredients in pan, bring to boil, simmer, uncovered, for about 8 minutes or until liquid has evaporated, stirring occasionally. Blend or process mixture until smooth; cool.

LEFT: Peanut Butter Bubble Cookies.
RIGHT: From back: Fig and Ginger Oaties, Spicy Wholemeal Apricot Slice.

Left: Jar and glasses from Shop 3, Balmain; cloth from Accoutrement

CORN FLAKE COCONUT CRUNCHIES

2 cups (60g) Corn Flakes, lightly crushed
2 cups self-raising flour
1 cup (50g) flaked coconut
1 cup (90g) coconut
1 cup brown sugar, firmly packed
2 eggs, lightly beaten
250g butter, melted

Combine Corn Flakes, sifted flour, both coconuts and sugar in large bowl. Stir in eggs and butter. Place level tablespoons of mixture about 5cm apart on greased oven trays. Bake in moderately hot oven for about 12 minutes or until lightly browned; cool on trays.
Makes about 40.

OAT BRAN DATE COOKIES

1 cup white self-raising flour
1 cup wholemeal self-raising flour
1 teaspoon ground nutmeg
1 cup (80g) Crunchy Oat Bran Cereal
1/2 cup brown sugar, firmly packed
100g butter, chopped
1 cup (160g) chopped dates
1 egg, lightly beaten
2/3 cup milk, approximately
2 tablespoons castor sugar

Sift flours and nutmeg into bowl, stir in bran and brown sugar, rub in butter. Stir in dates, egg and enough milk to give a soft consistency. Drop level tablespoons of mixture about 5cm apart onto greased oven trays, sprinkle with castor sugar. Bake in moderate oven for about 15 minutes or until cookies are lightly browned; cool on trays.
Makes about 35.

DATE AND BANANA SLICE

1/2 cup chopped dates
1/4 cup water
1 tablespoon honey
90g butter
3/4 cup raw sugar
1 cup self-raising flour
1/4 cup plain flour
1/2 teaspoon ground nutmeg
3/4 cup rice bran
1/3 cup mashed banana
ground nutmeg, extra
LEMON ICING
2½ cups icing sugar
30g soft butter
2 tablespoons lemon juice
1 tablespoon water, approximately

Grease 25cm x 30cm Swiss roll pan. Combine dates, water and honey in pan, bring to boil, simmer, uncovered, for 2 minutes or until slightly thickened; cool.

Beat butter and sugar in small bowl with electric mixer until combined. Stir in sifted flours and nutmeg, date mixture, bran and banana. Spread mixture evenly over base of prepared pan. Bake in moderate oven for about 30 minutes or until firm; stand 20 minutes. Spread with icing, sprinkle with a little extra nutmeg.
Lemon Icing: Sift icing sugar into small heatproof bowl, stir in butter and juice, and enough water to give a stiff paste. Stir over pan of simmering water until spreadable.

ABOVE: From left: Corn Flake Coconut Crunchies, Oat Bran Date Cookies. RIGHT: Date and Banana Slice.

Above: Bowls from Shop 3, Balmain; violet basket from Liquidamber Nursery

WHEATY YOGHURT SLICE

1 cup plain flour
½ cup self-raising flour
125g butter
½ cup castor sugar
1 egg, lightly beaten
⅔ cup lightly crushed Weet-Bix
⅓ cup All-Bran
TOPPING
2 x 200g cartons fruit salad yoghurt
⅓ cup castor sugar
2 eggs, lightly beaten

Grease 20cm x 30cm lamington pan, line base with paper; grease paper. Sift flours into bowl, rub in butter; stir in sugar and egg. Press mixture evenly over base of prepared pan. Bake in moderately hot oven for about 18 minutes or until lightly browned; cool.

Spread base with topping, sprinkle with combined Weet-Bix and All-Bran. Bake in moderate oven for about 40 minutes or until lightly browned and set. Cool in pan. Refrigerate for 30 minutes before cutting.
Topping: Combine all ingredients in bowl.

SEMOLINA ALMOND CRESCENTS

½ cup milk
150g butter
1 cup (170g) fine ground semolina
100g packaged almond paste, chopped
⅔ cup castor sugar
½ teaspoon almond essence
2 eggs
1½ cups plain flour
1 cup self-raising flour
1 cup (140g) slivered almonds, toasted, chopped
icing sugar

Combine milk and butter in pan, stir over low heat until butter is melted, gradually stir into semolina in bowl; cool, stirring mixture occasionally.

Beat almond paste, sugar, essence and eggs in small bowl with electric mixer on low speed until combined, increase to medium speed, beat further 2 minutes or until light and fluffy. Stir in semolina mixture. Transfer mixture to large bowl, stir in sifted flours and almonds. Turn onto lightly floured surface, knead lightly until smooth; cover, refrigerate for 30 minutes.

Roll 1½ level tablespoons of dough into an 8cm long sausage, shape into a crescent, place onto greased oven tray. Repeat with remaining dough, allowing about 3cm between crescents. Bake in moderate oven for about 20 minutes or until crisp and lightly browned, lift onto wire racks to cool. Dust cold crescents with sifted icing sugar.

Makes about 30.

BRAN AND APRICOT COOKIES

1 cup (70g) All-Bran
1 cup self-raising flour
1 cup (90g) coconut
½ cup brown sugar, firmly packed
½ cup chopped glace apricots
125g butter, melted
1 egg, lightly beaten

Combine All-Bran, sifted flour, coconut, sugar and apricots in bowl, stir in butter and egg. Place level tablespoons of mixture about 5cm apart on greased oven trays. Bake in moderately hot oven for about 10 minutes or until lightly browned; cool on trays.

Makes about 25.

LEFT: Wheaty Yoghurt Slice.
RIGHT: From back: Semolina Almond Crescents, Bran and Apricot Cookies.

China from Shop 3, Balmain

OATY NUT CRISPIES

125g butter
1 teaspoon vanilla essence
¾ cup brown sugar, firmly packed
1 egg
1½ cups (135g) rolled oats
¼ cup chopped pecans or walnuts
¾ cup self-raising flour

Beat butter, essence, sugar and egg in small bowl with electric mixer until light and fluffy. Stir in oats, nuts and sifted flour.

Using floured hands, roll 2 level teaspoons of mixture into a ball, place onto greased oven tray, flatten slightly.

Repeat with remaining mixture, allowing about 5cm between crispies. Bake in moderately hot oven for about 12 minutes or until lightly browned; cool on trays.

Makes about 45.

CINNAMON OAT BRAN CRISPS

2 egg whites
½ cup castor sugar
⅓ cup plain flour
1 teaspoon ground cinnamon
60g butter, melted
¼ cup rolled oats, finely chopped
2 tablespoons oat bran

Grease and flour oven trays, mark 5cm circles about 4cm apart on trays.

Beat egg whites in small bowl with electric mixer until soft peaks form. Gradually add sugar, beat until dissolved between each addition. Transfer mixture to large bowl, stir in sifted flour and cinnamon, butter, oats and bran.

Spread 2 level teaspoons of mixture onto a marked circle on prepared tray. Repeat with remaining mixture, baking about 4 at a time. Bake in moderate oven for about 12 minutes or until firm. Lift crisps carefully onto wire racks to cool.

Makes about 35.

MUESLI PASSIONFRUIT COOKIES

1 cup (130g) toasted muesli
1 cup (90g) coconut
⅔ cup self-raising flour
⅔ cup wheatgerm
½ cup rolled oats
⅔ cup raw sugar
2 tablespoons passionfruit pulp
180g butter, melted
1 egg, lightly beaten
⅔ cup coconut, extra

PASSIONFRUIT ICING
2 cups icing sugar
3 teaspoons soft butter
1 tablespoon water, approximately

Combine muesli, coconut, sifted flour, wheatgerm, oats and sugar in bowl. Strain passionfruit pulp, reserve juice for icing. Add passionfruit seeds to muesli mixture with butter and egg; mix well.

Place level tablespoons of mixture about 7cm apart on greased oven trays, flatten slightly. Bake in moderately hot oven for about 12 minutes or until lightly browned; cool on trays. Top cold cookies with icing, dip into extra coconut while icing is still soft.

Passionfruit Icing: Combine sifted icing sugar, butter and reserved passionfruit juice in heatproof bowl, add enough water to give a stiff paste. Stir over simmering water until spreadable.

Makes about 30.

CORN FLAKE GINGER CHEWS

3 cups (90g) Corn Flakes, crushed
¾ cup castor sugar
2 cups plain flour
3 teaspoons ground ginger
125g butter, melted
¼ cup golden syrup
¼ cup water
½ teaspoon bicarbonate of soda

ICING
30g butter
2 tablespoons golden syrup
1⅓ cups icing sugar
1 tablespoon boiling water

Grease 20cm x 30cm lamington pan. Combine Corn Flakes, sugar, sifted flour and ginger in bowl. Combine butter, golden syrup and water in pan, stir over low heat until butter is melted. Remove from heat, stir in soda, quickly stir into Corn Flake mixture, spread into prepared pan. Bake in moderate oven for about 25 minutes or until lightly browned. Stand for 10 minutes before spreading with icing. Cool in pan; cut when cold.

Icing: Combine butter and golden syrup in pan, stir over low heat until butter is melted. Remove from heat, stir in sifted icing sugar and water, stir until smooth.

LEFT: From left: Oaty Nut Crispies, Cinnamon Oat Bran Crisps.
BELOW: From left: Muesli Passionfruit Cookies, Corn Flake Ginger Chews.

WHEATGERM AND DATE TRIANGLES

⅔ cup dates
1½ cups plain flour
⅔ cup brown sugar, firmly packed
¾ cup wheatgerm
125g butter
2 egg yolks
1 tablespoon water, approximately

Cut dates into 1cm pieces. Combine sifted flour, sugar and wheatgerm in bowl, rub in butter. Add egg yolks and enough water to make ingredients cling together. Add dates, knead gently on lightly floured surface until dates are well combined.

Roll mixture into a log shape about 35cm long, shape log into a long triangle. Wrap in foil, refrigerate for 1 hour.

Remove foil from log, cut into 5mm slices, place about 2cm apart onto greased oven trays. Bake in moderate oven for about 12 minutes or until well browned. Stand for 5 minutes before lifting onto wire racks to cool.

Makes about 70.

SPICY WHOLEMEAL LEMON TWISTS

⅔ cup wholemeal plain flour
½ cup white plain flour
1 teaspoon mixed spice
¼ cup castor sugar
⅓ cup unprocessed bran
2 teaspoons grated lemon rind
90g butter, chopped
1 egg, lightly beaten
1 tablespoon unprocessed bran, extra
2 teaspoons raw sugar

Sift flours, spice and castor sugar into bowl, stir in bran and rind. Rub in butter (or process in food processor until just combined), stir in egg, mix to a firm dough. Knead dough on lightly floured surface until smooth; cover, refrigerate dough for 30 minutes.

Roll dough between sheets of greaseproof paper to 25cm x 30cm rectangle. Cut into 1½cm strips crossways, cut strips in half to measure 12½cm. Refrigerate for 15 minutes or until just firm.

Gently twist strips, sprinkle with combined extra bran and raw sugar. Place strips about 1cm apart on greased oven trays. Bake in moderately hot oven for about 10 minutes or until lightly browned. Cool on trays.

Makes about 50.

LEFT: From back: Spicy Wholemeal Lemon Twists, Wheatgerm and Date Triangles.
RIGHT: Peanut Butter Muesli Slice.
Right: Enamel ware from Country Collection

PEANUT BUTTER MUESLI SLICE

1 cup (130g) toasted muesli
½ cup rolled oats
¼ cup oat bran
¼ cup coconut
¼ cup wholemeal plain flour
¼ cup white self-raising flour
¼ cup unsalted roasted peanuts
125g butter
¼ cup crunchy peanut butter
¼ cup honey
¼ cup raw sugar

Grease 20cm x 30cm lamington pan. Combine muesli, oats, bran, coconut, sifted flours and nuts in bowl. Combine remaining ingredients in pan, stir over low heat until butter is melted, stir into dry ingredients. Spread mixture evenly into prepared pan, bake in moderate oven for about 20 minutes or until lightly browned. Cool in pan before cutting.

OAT AND CURRANT CRUNCHIES

125g butter
1 teaspoon grated lemon rind
½ cup demerara sugar
1 egg
¾ cup self-raising flour
⅔ cup rolled oats
½ cup oat bran
½ cup currants
2 tablespoons demerara sugar, extra

Beat butter, rind, sugar and egg in small bowl with electric mixer until just combined. Stir in sifted flour, oats, bran and currants. Place level tablespoons of mixture about 4cm apart on greased oven trays, sprinkle with extra sugar. Bake in moderately hot oven for about 12 minutes or until lightly browned; cool on trays.

Makes about 25.

BRAN AND MAPLE SYRUP COOKIES

180g butter
½ cup brown sugar, firmly packed
½ cup maple flavoured syrup
1½ cups plain flour
½ teaspoon ground cinnamon
2 cups (140g) All-Bran

Combine butter, sugar and syrup in pan, stir over low heat until butter is melted. Sift flour and cinnamon into large bowl, stir in All-Bran and butter mixture. Drop level tablespoons of mixture about 4cm apart onto greased oven trays. Bake in moderately hot oven for about 10 minutes or until browned; cool on wire racks.

Makes about 25.

LEFT : From left: Bran and Maple Syrup Cookies, Oat and Currant Crunchies.

China jars and plate from Accoutrement; flowers from Liquidamber Nursery

Beat butter and honey in small bowl with electric mixer until smooth, add eggs 1 at a time, beat until combined. Stir in sifted flours, bran and oil.

Spread mixture into prepared pan, bake in moderate oven for about 25 minutes or until well browned. Turn onto wire rack to cool. Spread with buttercream when cold.

Buttercream: Beat butter in small bowl with electric mixer until light and fluffy, add golden syrup and milk, beat until combined. Gradually beat in sifted icing sugar.

CORN FLAKE COCONUT CRISPS

125g butter
1 teaspoon vanilla essence
½ cup castor sugar
1 egg
½ cup coconut
½ cup sultanas
1 cup self-raising flour
2 cups (60g) Corn Flakes, lightly crushed

Beat butter, essence, sugar and egg in small bowl with electric mixer until light and fluffy. Stir in coconut, sultanas and sifted flour.

Roll 2 level teaspoons of mixture together into a ball, roll in Corn Flakes, place onto greased oven tray. Repeat with remaining mixture and Corn Flakes, allowing about 4cm between crisps. Bake in moderately hot oven for about 15 minutes or until lightly browned. Loosen crisps; cool on trays.

Makes about 40.

GOLDEN ENERGY NUTTIES

125g butter
1 teaspoon vanilla essence
½ cup castor sugar
1 egg
¾ cup self-raising flour
½ cup plain flour
2 tablespoons milk
1 cup (40g) Nutri-Grain
½ cup unsalted roasted peanuts, chopped

Beat butter, essence, sugar and egg in small bowl with electric mixer until light and fluffy. Stir in sifted flours and milk, then Nutri-Grain and nuts.

Drop 2 level teaspoons of mixture together onto greased oven tray. Repeat with remaining mixture, allowing about 5cm between cookies. Bake in moderately hot oven for about 10 minutes or until lightly browned; cool on trays.

Makes about 50.

OATY CHOCOLATE BARS

1½ cups (135g) rolled oats
1½ cups plain flour
¾ cup castor sugar
¾ cup chopped pecans or walnuts
¾ cup sultanas
¾ cup (140g) Choc Bits
180g butter, melted
¼ cup golden syrup

Lightly grease 20cm x 30cm lamington pan. Combine oats, sifted flour, sugar, nuts, sultanas and Choc Bits in large bowl, stir in butter and golden syrup. Press mixture evenly into prepared pan. Bake in moderate oven for about 25 minutes or until lightly browned; cool slice in pan before cutting.

BRAN AND HONEY BARS

125g butter
½ cup honey
2 eggs
¼ cup self-raising flour
¾ cup plain flour
¾ cup unprocessed bran
¼ cup oil
BUTTERCREAM
90g butter
2 tablespoons golden syrup
1 tablespoon milk
¾ cup icing sugar

Lightly grease 20cm x 30cm lamington pan, place strip of paper long enough to cover base and extend over 2 opposite ends, grease paper.

ABOVE LEFT: From front: Oaty Chocolate Bars, Bran and Honey Bars.
RIGHT: From left: Golden Energy Nutties, Corn Flake Coconut Crisps.

OATY BANANA COOKIES

1½ cups plain flour
½ teaspoon bicarbonate of soda
1 cup (90g) rolled oats
1 cup (80g) banana chips, chopped
½ cup castor sugar
125g butter, melted
2 tablespoons golden syrup
1 egg, lightly beaten

Sift flour and soda into bowl, stir in oats, banana chips and sugar, then combined butter, golden syrup and egg.

Drop 2 level teaspoons of mixture together onto greased oven tray. Repeat with remaining mixture, allowing about 4cm between cookies. Bake in moderately hot oven for 10 minutes or until lightly browned; cool on trays.

Makes about 45.

HARLEQUIN FRUIT COOKIES

125g butter
2 tablespoons castor sugar
1 egg
¾ cup self-raising flour
½ teaspoon ground cinnamon
1 cup (100g) crushed Weet-Bix
1 cup (165g) dried fruit medley
2 tablespoons raw sugar

Beat butter and castor sugar in small bowl with electric mixer until light and fluffy. Beat in egg; stir in sifted flour and cinnamon, then Weet-Bix and fruit medley.

Using floured hands, roll 1 level tablespoon of mixture into a ball, place onto greased oven tray, press lightly with fork; sprinkle with raw sugar. Repeat with remaining mixture, allowing about 3cm between cookies. Bake in moderately hot oven for about 15 minutes or until lightly browned; cool on trays.

Makes about 20.

BRAN AND PECAN COOKIES

125g butter
1 teaspoon vanilla essence
½ cup castor sugar
½ cup brown sugar, firmly packed
1 egg
1¼ cups self-raising flour
½ cup plain flour
¾ cup All-Bran
½ cup chopped pecans
½ cup (95g) Choc Bits

Beat butter, essence, sugars and egg in small bowl with electric mixer until smooth and creamy. Transfer mixture to large bowl, stir in sifted flours, All-Bran, nuts and Choc Bits.

Roll 2 level teaspoons of mixture into a ball, place onto greased oven tray. Repeat with remaining mixture, allowing about 3cm between cookies. Bake in moderate oven for about 15 minutes or until lightly browned; cool on wire racks.

Makes about 50.

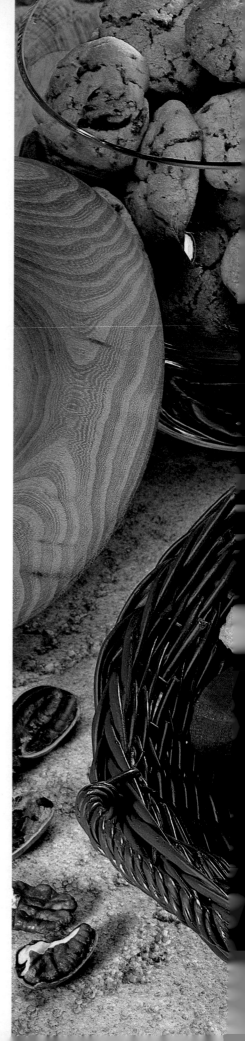

RIGHT: Clockwise from front: Oaty Banana Cookies, Bran and Pecan Cookies, Harlequin Fruit Cookies.

CARAMEL AND BUTTERSCOTCH

Like chocolate, caramel is one of the most popular flavours. There are different types of caramel but, when used in biscuits, cakes and slices, it generally indicates that brown sugar has been used. The sweet flavour can also come from honey, golden syrup and maple syrup.
Butterscotch is a very close cooking cousin to caramel, as it uses similar ingredients. Both can become delicious addictions! Now, turn to our "Hints for Success" at the back of this book for helpful tips.

CARAMEL, DATE AND WALNUT SLICE

1½ cups plain flour
125g butter
1 cup brown sugar, firmly packed
1 egg, lightly beaten
½ teaspoon bicarbonate of soda
½ cup cream
½ cup chopped dates
1 cup (100g) walnut pieces

Grease 20cm x 30cm lamington pan, cover base with paper, grease paper. Sift flour into bowl, rub in butter, stir in sugar. Press half the mixture firmly over base of prepared pan, bake in moderately hot oven for about 12 minutes or until lightly browned; cool.

Combine remaining flour mixture, egg, sifted soda, cream, dates and nuts in bowl; mix well. Pour mixture over base, bake in moderately hot oven for about 25 minutes or until topping is just firm. Cool in pan.

MAPLE SYRUP JUMBLES

90g butter
⅓ cup maple flavoured syrup
1½ tablespoons castor sugar
4 cups (120g) Corn Flakes
½ cup chopped unsalted roasted
    cashew nuts
¼ cup shredded coconut, toasted
1 tablespoon sesame seeds, toasted

Combine butter, syrup and sugar in pan, stir over low heat until butter is melted, boil, uncovered, for 2 minutes. Combine remaining ingredients in large bowl, gently stir in butter mixture. Drop level tablespoons of mixture into paper patty cases, place on oven trays. Bake in moderate oven for about 10 minutes or until lightly browned.

Makes about 40.

BUTTERSCOTCH GINGER CREAMS

250g butter
½ cup brown sugar, firmly packed
1¾ cups plain flour
2 teaspoons ground ginger
BUTTERSCOTCH CREAM
30g butter
1 tablespoon brown sugar
1 tablespoon cream
1 cup icing sugar

Beat butter and sugar in small bowl with electric mixer until light and fluffy. Transfer mixture to large bowl, stir in sifted flour and ginger. Spoon mixture into piping bag fitted with 2cm fluted tube. Pipe 2½cm stars about 3cm apart on greased oven trays, bake in moderate oven for about 10 minutes or until lightly browned; cool on trays.

Join biscuits with butterscotch cream; dust with sifted icing sugar, if desired.

Butterscotch Cream: Combine butter and brown sugar in pan, stir over low heat until sugar is dissolved and butter melted. Add cream, stir over heat until smooth. Remove from heat, gradually stir in sifted icing sugar; cool.

Makes about 85.

LEFT: From left: Butterscotch Ginger Creams, Maple Syrup Jumbles.
ABOVE: Caramel, Date and Walnut Slice.

Vase and plate from Shop 3, Balmain

BUTTERSCOTCH BUTTONS

125g butter
1 teaspoon vanilla essence
½ cup brown sugar, firmly packed
1 tablespoon golden syrup
1¼ cups self-raising flour

Beat butter, essence, sugar and golden syrup in small bowl with electric mixer until light and fluffy; stir in sifted flour. Roll level teaspoons of mixture into balls, place about 5cm apart onto greased oven trays, flatten slightly with a fork. Bake in slow oven for about 20 minutes or until firm. Cool on wire racks.

Makes about 75.

CHOCOLATE CARAMEL SLICE

200g packet Kingston biscuits
30g unsalted butter, melted
CARAMEL FILLING
500g packet soft Jersey caramels
60g unsalted butter
2 tablespoons milk
TOPPING
100g dark chocolate, melted
30g unsalted butter, melted

Line 23cm square slab pan with foil. Blend or process biscuits until fine, stir in butter. Press crumb mixture evenly over base of prepared pan, refrigerate while preparing caramel filling.

Spread filling evenly over base, refrigerate until firm. Spread evenly with topping, refrigerate until firm.
Caramel Filling: Combine caramels, butter and milk in pan, stir over low heat until caramels are melted. (A few white pieces will not dissolve.)
Topping: Combine chocolate and butter in small bowl.

GOLDEN SPICY JUMBLES

60g butter
½ cup brown sugar, firmly packed
¾ cup golden syrup
1 egg, lightly beaten
2½ cups plain flour
½ cup self-raising flour
½ teaspoon bicarbonate soda
1 teaspoon ground cinnamon
1 teaspoon ground cloves
2 teaspoons ground ginger
1 teaspoon mixed spice
ICING
1 egg white
1½ cups icing sugar
2 teaspoons plain flour
1 tablespoon lemon juice,
    approximately
pink food colouring

Combine butter, sugar and golden syrup in pan, stir over low heat until sugar is dissolved and butter melted; cool for 10 minutes. Transfer mixture to large bowl, stir in egg and sifted dry ingredients. Turn onto lightly floured surface, knead gently until mixture loses its stickiness; cover, refrigerate for 30 minutes.

Roll dough between sheets of greaseproof paper until 1cm thick. Cut 3½cm rounds from dough, place rounds about 3cm apart on greased oven trays. Bake in moderately hot oven for about 6 minutes or until lightly browned; cool on trays. Dip half of each biscuit into icing.
Icing: Lightly beat egg white in small bowl, gradually stir in sifted icing sugar and flour. Stir in enough juice to make a spreadable consistency. Tint with colouring. Keep icing covered with a damp cloth while it is in use.

Makes about 55.

RIGHT: Clockwise from back: Butterscotch Buttons, Chocolate Caramel Slice, Golden Spicy Jumbles.

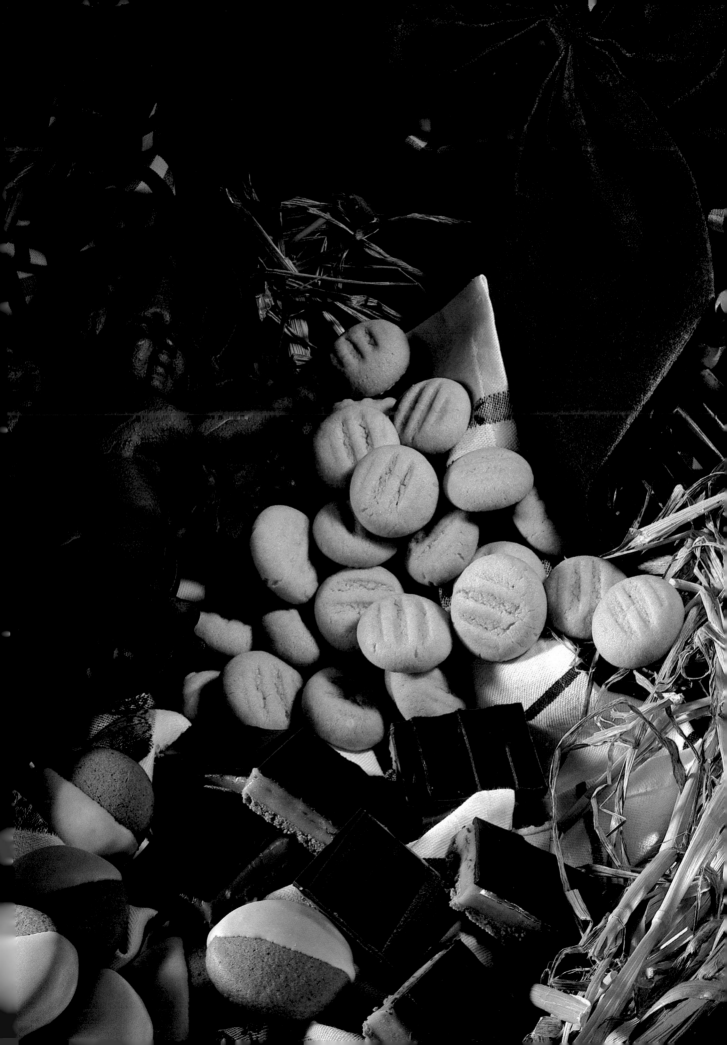

HONEY ALMOND FINGERS

60g butter
1/3 cup honey
1/3 cup golden syrup
1/2 cup packaged ground almonds
1 1/4 cups plain flour
1/2 teaspoon bicarbonate of soda
1/2 teaspoon ground ginger
1 tablespoon milk

HONEY ICING
1 1/3 cups icing sugar
2 tablespoons milk
1 tablespoon honey
1 teaspoon soft butter

Combine butter, honey and golden syrup in pan, stir over low heat until butter is melted, bring to boil, remove from heat; stand for 10 minutes. Stir in almonds, sifted dry ingredients and milk. Cover, stand at room temperature for about 2 hours or until mixture thickens.

Turn mixture onto floured surface, knead lightly until smooth. Divide mixture into quarters. Roll each quarter into a long 1cm thick sausage, cut into 6cm lengths, shape ends slightly.

Place fingers about 4cm apart onto greased oven trays, bake in moderate oven for about 8 minutes or until lightly coloured. Stand for 5 minutes before lifting onto wire racks to cool. Spread biscuits with icing, stand on racks until set.
Honey Icing: Sift icing sugar into bowl, stir in milk, honey and butter.

Makes about 55.

CARAMEL CHOCOLATE FUDGE BARS

2 x 200g packets Tim Tam chocolate
    biscuits
125g butter, melted
50g butter, extra
4 x 50g Chokito bars, chopped
2 x 100g packets white marshmallows
2 tablespoons milk
3 cups (90g) Rice Bubbles

Grease 20cm x 30cm lamington pan, line with baking paper. Blend or process biscuits until fine, add butter, mix well. Press mixture evenly over base of prepared pan; refrigerate until firm.

Combine extra butter, Chokito bars, marshmallows and milk in large pan, stir over low heat until marshmallows are melted and mixture combined. Stir in Rice Bubbles, spread evenly over base, refrigerate for several hours or overnight before cutting.

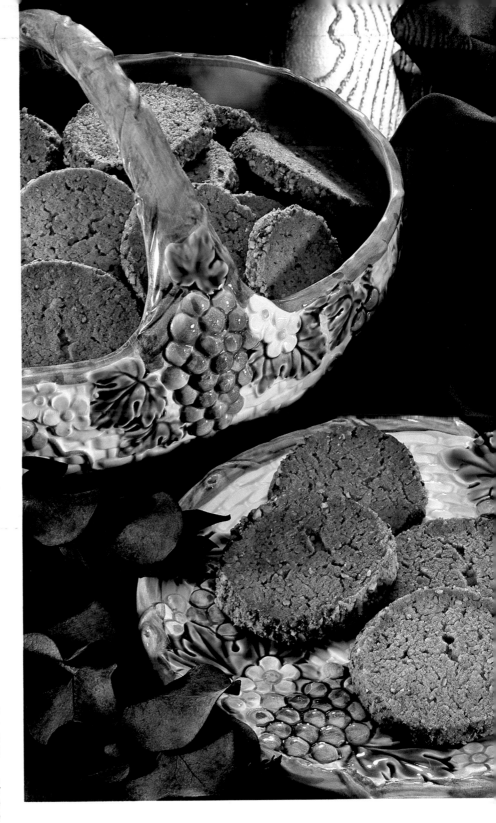

LEFT: From back: Caramel Chocolate Fudge Bars, Honey Almond Fingers.
ABOVE RIGHT: Butterscotch Pecan Cookies.

Above right: Dishes from China Doll

BUTTERSCOTCH PECAN COOKIES

1/2 cup pecans
225g packet Self Saucing
    Butterscotch Sponge Pudding
1/4 cup castor sugar
1 cup plain flour
100g butter, melted
2 tablespoons water, approximately
1/2 cup finely chopped pecans, extra

Blend or process pecans until finely ground, combine in bowl with pudding and sauce sachets, sugar and sifted flour. Stir in butter and enough water to mix to a firm dough, stand 5 minutes.

Shape dough into a log shape about 5cm in diameter. Roll log in extra pecans, wrap in foil, refrigerate for 1 hour. Remove foil, cut log into 4mm rounds, place rounds about 5cm apart onto greased oven trays. Bake in moderate oven for about 12 minutes or until well browned. Stand cookies for 5 minutes before lifting onto wire racks to cool.

Makes about 50.

CARAMEL NUTTY TRIANGLES

2 cups (250g) plain chocolate biscuit
    crumbs
180g butter, melted
90g butter, extra
1 cup sweetened condensed milk
¼ cup golden syrup
½ cup brown sugar, firmly packed
250g Picnic chocolate bars, chopped
½ cup crushed nuts

Lightly grease 20cm x 30cm lamington
pan. Combine crumbs and butter in bowl,
press evenly over base of prepared pan,
refrigerate until firm.

Combine extra butter, condensed milk,
golden syrup and sugar in pan, stir over
heat until boiling, boil, stirring, until mixture
is thickened and starts to leave the side
of pan.

Remove from heat, add Picnic bars,
stir until melted. Spread quickly over
prepared base, sprinkle with nuts, cool.
Refrigerate for several hours or overnight
before cutting.

CARAMEL BANANA PINWHEELS

60g butter
½ teaspoon vanilla essence
⅓ cup castor sugar
1 egg
1 cup self-raising flour
1 cup plain flour
¼ cup mashed banana
CARAMEL
40g butter
¼ cup brown sugar

Beat butter, essence and sugar in small
bowl with electric mixer until light and fluffy; add egg, beat until combined. Stir in
sifted flours and banana, mix to a firm
dough; cover, refrigerate for 30 minutes.

Roll half the dough between sheets of
greaseproof paper to 20cm x 30cm rectangle. Spread evenly with half the
caramel, roll up firmly from a long side.
Repeat with remaining dough and
caramel. Wrap rolls in foil, refrigerate for
30 minutes.

Cut rolls into 5mm slices, place about
2cm apart onto baking paper-covered
oven trays. Bake in moderate oven for
about 15 minutes or until lightly browned;
cool on trays.

Caramel: Beat butter in small bowl with
wooden spoon until smooth, add sugar;
beat until combined.

Makes about 85.

*RIGHT: From left: Caramel Banana
Pinwheels, Caramel Nutty Triangles.*

GIANT ORANGE AND CARAMEL COOKIES

125g butter
3 teaspoons grated orange rind
1½ cups brown sugar, firmly packed
1 egg
2 tablespoons orange juice
2¼ cups plain flour
½ cup self-raising flour
2 teaspoons mixed spice
1 egg white, lightly beaten
½ cup flaked almonds

Beat butter, rind and sugar in small bowl with electric mixer until light and fluffy. Add egg and orange juice, beat until combined. Transfer mixture to large bowl, stir in sifted dry ingredients.

Roll 2 level tablespoons of mixture into a ball, place onto greased oven tray, flatten until 5mm thick. Brush with egg white, sprinkle with almonds.

Repeat with remaining mixture, egg white and almonds, allowing 4 cookies per tray. Bake in moderate oven for about 15 minutes or until lightly browned; cool on wire racks.

Makes about 15.

CARAMEL CREAMS

250g butter
1 teaspoon vanilla essence
¾ cup brown sugar, firmly packed
1 egg yolk
2¼ cups plain flour

FILLING
20g butter
¼ cup cream
1½ cups icing sugar

Beat butter, essence, sugar and egg yolk in small bowl with electric mixer until smooth. Transfer mixture to large bowl, stir in sifted flour. Knead dough on lightly floured surface until smooth; cover, refrigerate for 30 minutes.

Roll dough between sheets of greaseproof paper until 5mm thick. Cut 4cm squares from dough. Place squares about 3cm apart on greased oven trays. Bake in moderate oven for about 12 minutes or until firm. Loosen biscuits, cool on trays. Join cold biscuits with filling.
Filling: Stir butter in pan over heat until lightly browned. Remove from heat, stir in cream and sifted icing sugar.

Makes about 55.

CARAMEL COCONUT SLICE

½ cup plain flour
½ cup self-raising flour
½ cup coconut
½ cup castor sugar
100g butter, melted
CARAMEL FILLING
400g can sweetened condensed milk
2 tablespoons golden syrup
¼ cup brown sugar
60g butter, melted
COCONUT TOPPING
2 eggs, lightly beaten
⅓ cup castor sugar
2 cups (180g) coconut

Grease 25cm x 30cm Swiss roll pan. Sift flours into bowl, stir in coconut, sugar and butter, press evenly over base of prepared pan. Bake in moderate oven for about 12 minutes or until lightly browned; cool.

Spread filling evenly over base, sprinkle with topping. Bake in moderate oven for about further 25 minutes or until topping is lightly browned; cool in pan.
Caramel Filling: Combine all ingredients in bowl; mix well.
Coconut Topping: Combine all the ingredients in bowl; mix well.

GOLDEN LACE SNAPS

125g butter
⅓ cup brown sugar
¼ cup glucose syrup
½ cup rolled oats
⅓ cup plain flour
2 tablespoons sour cream
1 teaspoon vanilla essence

Combine butter, sugar and glucose in heavy-based pan, stir over low heat until sugar is dissolved. Bring to boil, simmer, stirring, for about 8 minutes or until mixture is golden brown. Remove from heat, stir in oats, flour, cream and essence; cool.

Place level teaspoons of mixture about 10cm apart onto ungreased oven tray, flatten slightly. Baking 1 tray of biscuits at a time, bake in moderate oven for about 8 minutes or until lightly browned. Remove from oven; cool for 1 minute. Lift snaps from tray using metal spatula, roll immediately around handles of wooden spoons. Cool snaps on handles for 1 minute before placing on wire rack to cool completely.

Makes about 45.

LEFT: Giant Orange and Caramel Cookies.
RIGHT: Clockwise from front: Caramel Coconut Slice, Golden Lace Snaps, Caramel Creams.
Right: Plates from Corso de Fiori

ICED CARAMEL NUT COOKIES

125g butter
2/3 cup brown sugar, firmly packed
2 tablespoons golden syrup
2 egg yolks
2 1/2 cups self-raising flour
1/2 teaspoon bicarbonate of soda
2/3 cup chopped walnuts or pecans
CARAMEL ICING
30g butter
1/4 cup brown sugar
2 tablespoons cream
1 cup icing sugar

Beat butter, sugar, golden syrup and egg yolks in small bowl with electric mixer until light and fluffy. Transfer mixture to large bowl, stir in sifted dry ingredients and nuts in 2 batches.

Roll 1 level tablespoon of mixture into a ball, place on greased oven tray. Repeat with remaining mixture, allowing about 5cm between cookies. Bake in moderate oven for about 20 minutes or until well browned; cool on trays.

Dip top of each cookie in warm icing, place onto wire rack until set.
Caramel Icing: Combine butter and sugar in pan, stir over heat until butter is melted and sugar dissolved. Stir in cream, bring to boil, remove from heat, gradually stir in sifted icing sugar.

Makes about 35.

SPICY SOUR CREAM TWISTS

1/2 cup self-raising flour
2 1/2 cups plain flour
1 teaspoon mixed spice
1/2 teaspoon ground cinnamon
1/2 teaspoon ground ginger
1/2 cup brown sugar, firmly packed
1/2 cup golden syrup
1/2 cup sour cream
125g butter, melted
1/4 cup icing sugar
1/2 teaspoon ground cinnamon, extra

Sift flours, spices and brown sugar into large bowl, stir in combined golden syrup, cream and butter; mix to a firm dough.

Turn dough onto lightly floured surface, knead gently until smooth; cover, refrigerate for 30 minutes.

Roll 2 level teaspoons of dough into a thin roll about 20cm long. Hold roll in centre, twist ends together, place on greased oven tray. Repeat with remaining dough, allowing about 2cm between twists. Bake in moderate oven for about 18 minutes or until lightly browned; cool on wire racks.

Dust lightly with sifted icing sugar and extra cinnamon.

Makes about 75.

BELOW: From back: Iced Caramel Nut Cookies, Spicy Sour Cream Twists. RIGHT: Caramel Cream Ginger Snaps. Below: China from Sydney Antique Centre. Right: China from The Country Trader

CARAMEL CREAM GINGER SNAPS

¼ cup golden syrup
90g butter
⅓ cup brown sugar
½ cup plain flour
2 teaspoons ground ginger

FILLING
40g butter
¾ cup brown sugar, firmly packed
½ cup cream
1 tablespoon cornflour
1 tablespoon water
⅔ cup cream, extra

Combine golden syrup, butter and sugar in pan, stir until butter is melted and sugar dissolved. Remove from heat; stir in sifted flour and ginger. Drop level teaspoons of mixture about 8cm apart onto greased oven trays, about 4 on each tray. Baking 1 tray at a time, bake in moderate oven for about 5 minutes or until lightly browned. Remove from oven, cool on tray for 1 minute. Lift snaps from tray using metal spatula, roll immediately around handles of wooden spoons. Cool snaps on handles for 1 minute before placing on wire racks to cool completely.

Spoon filling into piping bag fitted with small plain tube, pipe filling into centre of each snap. Pipe extra cream into ends of each snap.

Filling: Melt butter in pan, stir in sugar and cream. Stir until sugar is dissolved, stir in blended cornflour and water. Stir over heat until mixture boils and thickens. Simmer for 6 minutes, stirring occasionally. Remove from heat; cover, cool. Refrigerate filling until thick. Whip extra cream until thick, spoon into piping bag fitted with small fluted tube.

Makes about 40.

CRUNCHY HONEYCOMB SNAPS

90g butter
1/3 cup brown sugar
1/4 cup honey
1 1/3 cups plain flour
2 x 45g bars chocolate-coated
    honeycomb, finely chopped

Combine butter, sugar and honey in pan, stir over low heat until butter is melted. Stir in sifted flour, cool to room temperature.

Turn dough onto floured surface, knead in honeycomb. Roll 2 level teaspoons of mixture into a ball, place onto baking paper-covered oven tray, flatten slightly. Repeat with remaining mixture, allowing about 5cm between snaps. Bake in moderate oven for about 15 minutes or until browned; cool on trays.

Makes about 35.

ALMOND PRALINE BISCUITS

1 cup castor sugar
1/3 cup water
1 cup (125g) slivered almonds,
    toasted
90g butter
1/3 cup brown sugar
1 egg
1 cup plain flour
1/4 cup self-raising flour
CARAMEL
1/2 cup sweetened condensed milk
3 teaspoons butter
1 tablespoon golden syrup

Combine castor sugar and water in pan, stir over heat, without boiling, until sugar is dissolved. Bring to boil, boil, uncovered, without stirring, for about 5 minutes or until deep golden colour; pour over almonds on well-greased oven tray, cool.

When almond toffee is set, crush with rolling pin or meat mallet. Reserve 1/3 cup almond praline mixture.

Beat butter, brown sugar and egg in small bowl with electric mixer until light and fluffy. Stir in sifted flours and praline. Turn dough onto lightly floured surface, knead until well combined; cover, refrigerate for 30 minutes.

Roll dough between sheets of greaseproof paper until 2mm thick, cut into 3 1/2cm squares, place about 2cm apart on baking paper-covered oven trays. Bake in moderate oven for about 6 minutes or until lightly browned; cool biscuits on trays.

Sandwich biscuits with 1/2 level teaspoon of caramel, place 1/4 level teaspoon of caramel on top of each biscuit, press on reserved praline.
Caramel: Combine all ingredients in pan, stir over heat until mixture boils. Boil, stirring, for about 3 minutes or until light caramel colour; cool.

Makes about 45.

CARAMEL NUT ROUNDS

3/4 cup plain flour
1 tablespoon custard powder
1 tablespoon icing sugar
60g butter
2 teaspoons water, approximately
CARAMEL NUT TOPPING
1/3 cup blanched almonds
1/3 cup unroasted hazelnuts
1/3 cup pecans or walnuts
1/3 cup castor sugar
3 teaspoons glucose syrup
1 1/2 tablespoons water
2 tablespoons cream

Sift flour, custard powder and icing sugar into bowl, rub in butter. Stir in enough water to make ingredients cling together. Turn onto floured surface, knead until smooth; cover, refrigerate for 30 minutes.

Roll dough between sheets of greaseproof paper until 3mm thick. Cut into 4cm rounds, place about 2cm apart on greased oven trays. Bake in moderately hot oven for about 10 minutes or until lightly browned; cool on trays. Place a level teaspoon of topping onto each round, stand at room temperature until topping is set.
Caramel Nut Topping: Chop nuts all about the same size, toast on oven tray in moderate oven for about 5 minutes or until lightly browned.

Combine sugar, glucose and water in pan, stir over heat, without boiling, until sugar is dissolved. Bring to boil, boil, without stirring, for about 2 minutes or until golden brown. Gently stir in cream and nuts; use immediately.

Makes about 45.

RIGHT: From back: Crunchy Honeycomb Snaps, Almond Praline Biscuits, Caramel Nut Rounds.

Plate from Studio-Haus

COCONUT

Multi-function coconut's greatest asset is that it goes so well with everything. It mixes easily with nuts, chocolate, spices, fruit (particularly lemon), whatever you like best. As well as flavour, it lends a tender moistness to biscuits and slices, which usually keep well as a result. Although there are different types of coconut, we have used desiccated coconut unless otherwise specified in individual recipes. Now, for helpful cooking guidelines, turn to our "Hints for Success" section at the back of this book.

RASPBERRY COCONUT RINGS

125g butter
1 cup castor sugar
1 egg
1 cup plain flour
1 cup self-raising flour
½ cup coconut
½ cup raspberry jam
½ cup coconut, extra
TOPPING
100g packet pink marshmallows
30g butter
1 tablespoon milk
60g white chocolate, chopped

Beat butter, sugar and egg in small bowl with electric mixer until light and fluffy. Stir in sifted flours and coconut. Knead gently on lightly floured surface until smooth; cover, refrigerate for 30 minutes.

Roll dough between sheets of greaseproof paper until 3mm thick. Cut

5cm rounds from dough. Cut 2cm centres from half the rounds. Place rounds and rings about 3cm apart on greased oven trays. Bake in moderate oven for about 10 minutes or until lightly browned; cool on wire racks.

Spread rounds with jam, spread rings with topping, dip into extra coconut; top rounds with rings.

Topping: Combine marshmallows, butter and milk in pan, stir over low heat until marshmallows are melted. Remove from heat, add chocolate, stir until smooth.

Makes about 40.

COCONUT FORTUNE COOKIES

2 egg whites
⅓ cup icing sugar
1 teaspoon coconut essence
30g butter, melted
⅓ cup plain flour
¼ cup coconut, toasted

Grease and lightly flour oven trays, mark 2 x 8cm circles on each tray.

Beat egg whites in small bowl with electric mixer until just foamy, gradually beat in sifted icing sugar, essence and butter. Stir in sifted flour, mix until smooth. Place a level teaspoon of mixture in centre of each marked circle on trays, spread evenly to cover circles completely, sprinkle evenly with a little coconut.

Baking 1 tray at a time, bake in moderate oven for about 5 minutes or until lightly browned around the edges, remove from oven. Working quickly, lift cookies from tray, fold in half, then lightly bend each cookie over rim of a glass, cool for 30 seconds. Place cookies on wire rack to complete cooling. Repeat with remaining cookie mixture and coconut.

Makes about 45.

BELOW LEFT: Raspberry Coconut Rings.
BELOW: Coconut Fortune Cookies.

Below left: China from Villeroy & Boch; tiles from Country Floors

COCONUT GINGER CREAMS

180g butter
⅔ cup castor sugar
1 egg
1¼ cups plain flour
½ cup self-raising flour
¾ cup coconut
GINGER CREAM
60g butter
1 tablespoon golden syrup
¾ cup icing sugar
1 teaspoon ground ginger

Beat butter, sugar and egg in small bowl with electric mixer until light and fluffy. Transfer mixture to large bowl, stir in sifted flours and coconut.

Spoon mixture into piping bag fitted with fluted tube. Pipe 4cm rounds about 4cm apart on greased oven trays. Bake in moderate oven for about 12 minutes or until lightly browned. Cool biscuits on trays for 10 minutes before lifting onto wire racks to cool completely. Sandwich biscuits with ginger cream.

Ginger Cream: Beat butter and golden syrup in small bowl with electric mixer until light and creamy, gradually beat in sifted icing sugar and ginger.

Makes about 45.

COCONUT APPLE CRUMBLE SLICE

100g butter
½ cup castor sugar
1 cup plain flour
¾ cup coconut
1¼ cups canned pie apples
TOPPING
½ cup plain flour
1 teaspoon ground cinnamon
30g butter
¼ cup castor sugar

Grease 20cm x 30cm lamington pan. Beat butter and sugar in bowl with electric mixer until light and fluffy. Stir in sifted flour and coconut. Press mixture evenly over base of prepared pan. Bake in moderately hot oven for about 12 minutes or until lightly browned; cool.

Spread base evenly with apple, sprinkle with topping. Bake in moderate oven for about 35 minutes or until lightly browned; cool in pan.

Topping: Sift flour and cinnamon into bowl, rub in butter; stir in sugar.

RIGHT: From left: Coconut Ginger Creams, Coconut Apple Crumble Slice.

Plates from Powder Blue

COCONUT CUSTARD SLICE

1 cup self-raising flour
¾ cup plain flour
1½ cups (135g) coconut
¾ cup castor sugar
180g butter, melted
CUSTARD FILLING
2 tablespoons custard powder
2 tablespoons castor sugar
1¼ cups milk
20g butter
1 teaspoon vanilla essence

Grease 20cm x 30cm lamington pan. Sift flours into bowl, stir in coconut, sugar and butter; stir until ingredients cling together. Wrap one-third of mixture in foil, freeze for 30 minutes.

Press remaining mixture evenly over base of prepared pan, bake in moderately hot oven for about 15 minutes or until lightly browned; cool.

Spread filling evenly over base. Coarsely grate frozen mixture over custard; press gently into custard. Bake in moderate oven for about 25 minutes or until lightly browned. Cool in pan

Custard Filling: Blend custard powder and sugar in pan with ¼ cup of the milk until smooth, stir in remaining milk. Stir over heat until custard boils and thickens. Remove from heat, stir in butter and essence, cover surface with plastic wrap, cool to room temperature.

COCONUT CHOC CHERRY SLICE

2 cups (250g) plain chocolate
**   biscuit crumbs**
150g butter, melted
¾ cup castor sugar
⅓ cup milk
1⅔ cups (150g) coconut
1 egg white, lightly beaten
¼ cup icing sugar
¾ cup red glace cherries, finely
**   chopped**
TOPPING
200g dark chocolate, melted
60g butter, melted

Line 20cm x 30cm lamington pan with foil, lightly grease foil. Combine biscuit crumbs and butter in bowl, press evenly over base of prepared pan; refrigerate for 20 minutes or until firm.

Combine sugar and milk in small pan, stir over low heat until sugar is dissolved; cool for 5 minutes.

Transfer milk mixture to large bowl, stir in coconut, egg white, sifted icing sugar and cherries. Spread over prepared base; cover, refrigerate for 15 minutes. Spread topping over filling, refrigerate for several hours or overnight before cutting.

Topping: Combine chocolate and butter in bowl; stir until smooth.

LEFT: From left: Coconut Choc Cherry Slice, Coconut Custard Slice.

China from The Bay Tree

MOIST COCONUT CHOCOLATE SQUARES

90g butter
¼ cup castor sugar
2 egg yolks
¼ cup coconut
1¼ cups plain flour
2 tablespoons cocoa
100g dark chocolate, melted
15g butter, melted, extra

FILLING
¼ cup castor sugar
1½ tablespoons milk
¾ cup coconut
1 egg white, lightly beaten

Beat butter, sugar and egg yolks in small bowl with electric mixer until light and fluffy. Add coconut and sifted flour and cocoa, mix to a firm dough. Knead gently on lightly floured surface until smooth; cover, refrigerate for 30 minutes.

Roll dough on lightly floured surface until 3mm thick. Cut into 3½cm squares. Place squares about 3cm apart onto greased oven trays. Bake in moderate oven for about 10 minutes or until lightly browned; cool on trays. Sandwich biscuits with ½ level teaspoon of filling, spread tops with combined chocolate and extra butter; stand until set.

Filling: Combine sugar and milk in small pan, stir over low heat until sugar is dissolved. Remove from heat, combine with coconut and egg white in bowl.

Makes about 30.

COCONUT PINEAPPLE SLICE

125g butter
½ cup brown sugar, firmly packed
1½ cups plain flour

TOPPING
2 eggs
1 cup brown sugar, firmly packed
2 tablespoons plain flour
½ cup shredded coconut
⅓ cup slivered almonds, toasted
½ cup crushed pineapple, drained

Lightly grease 20cm x 30cm lamington pan, line with paper, grease paper. Beat butter and sugar in small bowl with electric mixer until light and fluffy. Stir in sifted flour, press evenly over base of prepared pan. Bake in moderately hot oven for about 15 minutes or until lightly browned; cool.

Pour topping evenly over base, bake in moderate oven for about 30 minutes or until lightly browned and firm; cool in pan. Refrigerate for 3 hours before cutting.

Topping: Whisk eggs, sugar and flour in bowl, stir in remaining ingredients.

SPICY COCONUT LEMON CRESCENTS

125g butter
2 teaspoons grated lemon rind
1 cup castor sugar
1 egg
½ cup coconut
1 tablespoon lemon juice
2½ cups self-raising flour
1 teaspoon ground cinnamon
1 teaspoon mixed spice
2 egg whites, lightly beaten
1½ cups (135g) coconut, extra

Beat butter, rind, sugar and egg in small bowl with electric mixer until light and fluffy. Stir in coconut and juice, then sifted flour and spices.

Roll 2 level teaspoons of mixture into a crescent shape, dip into egg whites, then roll in extra coconut. Place onto greased oven tray. Repeat with remaining mixture, egg whites and extra coconut, allowing about 4cm between crescents. Bake in moderate oven for about 15 minutes or until lightly browned; cool on trays.

Makes about 50.

LEFT: Clockwise from front: Moist Coconut Chocolate Squares, Spicy Coconut Lemon Crescents, Coconut Pineapple Slice.

China from Villeroy & Boch; tiles from Country Floors

COCONUT MOCHA SLICE

1 cup (90g) coconut
½ cup self-raising flour
⅓ cup brown sugar
100g butter
2 tablespoons coconut, extra

MOCHA TOPPING
2 teaspoons dry instant coffee
1 tablespoon hot water
400g can sweetened condensed milk
100g milk chocolate, grated
30g butter

Grease 20cm x 30cm lamington pan. Combine coconut, sifted flour and sugar in bowl, rub in butter. Press mixture firmly over base of prepared pan, bake in moderately hot oven for about 12 minutes or until lightly browned. Stand base 10 minutes before pouring over hot topping, sprinkle with extra coconut; cool to room temperature. Refrigerate overnight.

Mocha Topping: Dissolve coffee in water in pan, add remaining ingredients. Stir over low heat until chocolate and butter are melted. Bring to the boil, simmer, un-covered, stirring, for about 3 minutes or until mixture coats base of pan.

COCONUT MUESLI SNOWIES

1¼ cups (190g) toasted muesli
1 cup self-raising flour
1 cup (90g) coconut
1 cup (125g) unsalted roasted peanuts
½ cup castor sugar
125g butter, melted
1 egg, lightly beaten
1⅔ cups (250g) White Melts, melted
½ cup coconut, extra

Combine muesli, sifted flour, coconut, nuts and sugar in bowl, stir in butter and egg, stir until combined.

Place 2 level teaspoons of mixture together onto greased oven tray. Repeat with remaining mixture, allowing about 3cm between cookies. Bake in moderate oven for about 15 minutes or until lightly browned. Stand on trays for 5 minutes before lifting onto wire racks to cool. Dip tops of biscuits into White Melts, then extra coconut; place on wire racks to set.

Makes about 55.

LEMON AND HONEY COCONUT SLICE

1 cup self-raising flour
1 cup plain flour
1 teaspoon ground cinnamon
1 teaspoon grated lemon rind
2 tablespoons coconut
2 tablespoons castor sugar
125g butter
¼ cup honey
2 tablespoons lemon juice
1 tablespoon castor sugar, extra
½ teaspoon ground cinnamon, extra

LEMON FILLING
1 cup (90g) coconut
½ cup lemon butter
½ cup sweetened condensed milk

Grease 20cm x 30cm lamington pan. Sift flours and cinnamon into large bowl, stir in rind, coconut and sugar. Combine butter, honey and juice in pan, stir over heat until butter is melted, stir into dry ingredients. Wrap one-third of dough in foil, freeze for 15 minutes.

Press remaining dough over base of prepared pan, bake in moderate oven for about 12 minutes or until lightly browned.

Stand base for 10 minutes before spreading evenly with filling.

Coarsely grate frozen dough over filling, sprinkle with combined extra sugar and extra cinnamon. Bake slice in moderate oven for about 25 minutes or until lightly browned.
Filling: Combine all ingredients in bowl.

LEFT: Coconut Mocha Slice.
ABOVE: From left: Lemon and Honey Coconut Slice, Coconut Muesli Snowies.

Above: Plate and barrel from Appley Hoare Antiques

COCONUT LEMON TWISTS

90g butter
1 teaspoon grated lemon rind
⅓ cup castor sugar
1 egg
1 tablespoon lemon juice
1⅓ cups self-raising flour
⅓ cup custard powder
1 cup (90g) coconut
LEMON ICING
1½ cups icing sugar
20g soft butter
2 tablespoons lemon juice

Beat butter, rind, sugar and egg in small bowl with electric mixer until light and fluffy. Transfer to large bowl. Stir in juice, sifted flour and custard powder, then coconut.

Roll 2 level teaspoons of mixture into sausage shape about 12cm long. Fold sausage in half. Hold folded end, twist pieces together; place on greased oven tray. Repeat with remaining mixture, allowing about 5cm between twists. Bake in moderate oven for about 12 minutes or until lightly browned; cool on wire rack.

Dip ends of twists into icing; stand on racks until set.
Lemon Icing: Sift icing sugar into heatproof bowl, stir in butter and juice, stir over hot water until smooth.

Makes about 40.

SHREDDED COCONUT CHEWS

1 cup self-raising flour
1 cup (70g) shredded coconut
1 cup (30g) Corn Flakes
⅓ cup chopped glace apricots
¼ cup castor sugar
1 egg, lightly beaten
75g butter, melted

Sift flour into bowl, stir in coconut, Corn Flakes, apricots and sugar, add egg and butter, mix gently with fork until combined. Shape 2 level teaspoons of mixture into a ball, flatten slightly, place onto greased oven tray. Repeat with remaining mixture, allowing about 5cm between chews. Bake in moderately hot oven for about 12 minutes or until lightly browned and firm; cool on trays.

Makes about 35.

MILK CHOCOLATE COCONUT DREAMS

125g butter, melted
1 teaspoon vanilla essence
½ cup castor sugar
1 egg
1½ cups self-raising flour
2 tablespoons cocoa
½ cup coconut
125g Milk Melts, melted
1 cup (90g) coconut, extra

Combine butter, essence, sugar and egg in bowl, stir until combined. Stir in sifted flour and cocoa, then coconut. Roll 2 level teaspoons of dough into a ball, place onto greased oven tray. Repeat with remaining mixture, allowing about 5cm between cookies. Bake in moderate oven for about 15 minutes or until lightly browned; cool on wire racks.

Dip tops of cookies into Milk Melts, then extra coconut, stand until set.

Makes about 35.

RIGHT: Clockwise from back: Shredded Coconut Chews, Coconut Lemon Twists, Milk Chocolate Coconut Dreams.

COCONUT PINEAPPLE SNAILS

90g butter
1 teaspoon grated lemon rind
⅓ cup icing sugar
1 egg
¾ cup self-raising flour
⅔ cup plain flour
COCONUT PINEAPPLE FILLING
½ cup finely chopped glace
    pineapple
⅓ cup coconut
2 tablespoons marmalade

Beat butter, rind, sifted icing sugar and egg in small bowl with electric mixer until light and creamy. Stir in sifted flours. Knead on floured surface until smooth; cover, refrigerate for 30 minutes.

Roll dough between sheets of greaseproof paper to 25cm x 40cm rectangle. Remove top sheet of paper, carefully spread filling over dough, leaving 1cm border. Using bottom sheet of paper as a guide, roll up dough tightly from a long side to enclose filling, wrap roll in foil,

refrigerate for 30 minutes.

Remove foil from roll, cut roll into 1cm slices. Place about 2cm apart on greased oven trays. Bake in moderate oven for about 15 minutes or until lightly browned. Stand for 5 minutes before lifting onto wire racks to cool completely.
Filling: Combine all ingredients in bowl.
Makes about 35.

COCONUT CHOCOLATE ROUNDABOUTS

150g butter
1 teaspoon vanilla essence
⅔ cup castor sugar
1 egg
2 cups plain flour
¾ cup coconut
50g dark chocolate, melted

Beat butter, essence, sugar and egg in small bowl with electric mixer until light and fluffy. Transfer to large bowl, stir in sifted flour and coconut.

Divide dough into 5 portions. Knead 3

portions together on lightly floured surface until smooth. Add cooled chocolate to remaining 2 portions, knead together on lightly floured surface until smooth.

Shape plain dough into 4cm diameter log, about 22cm long. Roll chocolate dough between sheets of greaseproof paper to 18cm x 24cm rectangle. Place log on chocolate dough, wrap dough around log, smooth join with fingers. Wrap log in foil, freeze for 30 minutes.

Remove foil, cut log into 5mm slices, place slices about 2cm apart onto greased oven trays, bake in moderate oven for about 10 minutes or until lightly browned. Loosen biscuits, cool on trays.

Makes about 35.

LEFT: Coconut Pineapple Snails.
ABOVE: Coconut Chocolate Roundabouts.
Above: Plate from Amy's Tableware

COCONUT GEMS WITH DARK CHOCOLATE FILLING

3 egg whites
2 cups (180g) coconut
¾ cup castor sugar
1 tablespoon plain flour
FILLING
60g dark chocolate, melted
50g butter, melted

Beat egg whites in small bowl with electric mixer until firm peaks form. Fold in coconut, sugar and sifted flour, press mixture firmly together.

Using wet hands, roll level teaspoons of mixture into balls, place about 2cm apart on greased oven trays, flatten slightly. Bake in moderate oven for about 15 minutes or until lightly coloured. Stand gems on trays for 5 minutes before lifting onto wire racks to cool. Sandwich gems with filling.

Filling: Combine chocolate and butter in small bowl, cool to room temperature.

Makes about 30.

LAMINGTON DROPS

150g dark chocolate
125g butter
¼ cup brown sugar
1 egg, lightly beaten
½ cup coconut
1¼ cups plain flour
¼ cup self-raising flour
1 cup (90g) coconut, extra

Combine chocolate, butter and sugar in pan, stir over low heat until chocolate and butter are melted; cool for 5 minutes. Stir in egg, coconut and sifted flours. Cover, refrigerate for 30 minutes.

Roll 2 level teaspoons of mixture into a ball, roll in extra coconut, place on greased oven tray, flatten slightly. Repeat with remaining mixture and extra coconut, allowing about 2cm between drops. Bake in moderate oven for about 15 minutes or until coconut is lightly coloured, stand drops for 5 minutes before lifting onto wire racks to cool.

Makes about 40.

LEFT: From left: Coconut Gems With Dark Chocolate Filling, Lamington Drops.

SAVOURY

Tasty bites like these are terrific to have on hand to serve with drinks or for family eating. The savoury tastes will be popular with kids and adults alike, and recipes make lots for low costs. About half are cheesy, some are salty and others will be crispy golden surprises. All keep well in airtight containers, making it easy to have them on stand-by. First, though, turn to our "Hints for Success" at the back of this book for cooking information.

SESAME CHEESE STARS

1 cup plain flour
pinch cayenne pepper
60g butter
¾ cup grated tasty cheese
1 tablespoon grated parmesan
  cheese
½ cup cooked mashed potato
1 egg yolk
⅓ cup sesame seeds

Sift flour and pepper into bowl, rub in butter. Stir in cheeses, potato and egg yolk. Knead gently on floured surface until smooth; cover, refrigerate 30 minutes.

Roll dough on lightly floured surface until 3mm thick. Cut into 5cm stars, press stars into seeds, place stars seed-side-up about 1cm apart onto greased oven trays. Bake in moderate oven for about 15 minutes or until lightly browned. Cool on wire racks.

Makes about 100.

CURRY CARAWAY CRACKERS

1 tablespoon curry powder
1¼ cups plain flour
¼ cup self-raising flour
100g butter
1 egg, lightly beaten
1 teaspoon water, approximately
1 egg white, lightly beaten
salt
caraway seeds

Place curry powder in dry pan, stir over low heat until fragrant; cool. Sift flours and curry powder into bowl; rub in butter. Stir in egg and enough water to mix to a firm dough. Knead on floured surface until smooth; cover, refrigerate 30 minutes.

Roll dough between sheets of greaseproof paper until 2mm thick. Cut into 5cm rounds, place about 3cm apart onto greased oven trays. Brush lightly with a little egg white, sprinkle lightly with salt and caraway seeds. Bake in moderate oven for about 12 minutes or until lightly browned. Cool on trays.

Makes about 70.

LEFT: From left: Curry Caraway Crackers, Sesame Cheese Stars.
Plates from Amy's Tableware

CHEESE AND BACON BITES

3 bacon rashers, chopped
125g butter
1 cup (125g) grated tasty cheese
2 tablespoons grated parmesan
** cheese**
1 cup plain flour
¼ cup cornmeal
½ cup finely grated tasty
** cheese, extra**
2 teaspoons poppy seeds

Stir bacon over heat in pan until crisp; drain on absorbent paper. Beat butter in small bowl with electric mixer until light and creamy; beat in cheeses, beat until combined. Stir in sifted flour, cornmeal and bacon; mix well.

Shape 1½ level teaspoons of mixture into a ball, place onto greased oven tray, flatten slightly. Repeat with remaining mixture, allowing about 3cm between biscuits. Sprinkle with extra cheese and poppy seeds. Bake in moderately hot oven for about 15 minutes or until lightly browned; cool on trays.

Makes about 35.

FENNEL AND OLIVE PILLOWS

1 cup plain flour
100g butter
¼ cup unprocessed bran
2 tablespoons milk, approximately
1 tablespoon fennel seeds
FILLING
1 teaspoon butter
1 tablespoon finely chopped onion
¼ cup finely chopped fennel bulb
¼ cup pitted black olives, finely
** chopped**
1 tablespoon chopped fresh fennel
** leaves**
2 tablespoons packaged
** breadcrumbs**
1 tablespoon milk

Sift flour into bowl, rub in butter, stir in bran. Add enough milk to make a firm dough. Knead gently on floured surface until smooth; cover, refrigerate 30 minutes.

Roll pastry on lightly floured surface until 3mm thick. Cut pastry into 6cm x 7cm rectangles, place 1 level teaspoon of filling onto centre of each rectangle, brush edges with water. Roll rectangles up from short sides, with seams underneath; seal ends to form pillows. Brush with a little water, sprinkle with seeds. Bake in moderately hot oven for about 15 minutes or until well browned; cool on trays.
Filling: Heat butter in pan, add onion and fennel bulb, cook for 8 minutes over low heat. Add olives, cook, covered, further 8 minutes; remove from heat, stir in fennel leaves, breadcrumbs and milk; cool.

Makes about 15.

TOMATO BASIL CRACKERS

1¼ cups plain flour
30g butter
2 tablespoons chopped fresh basil
2 tablespoons tomato paste
¼ teaspoon ground black pepper
2 tablespoons water, approximately
1 egg white, lightly beaten
2 teaspoons sea salt

Sift flour into bowl, rub in butter. Stir in basil, paste and pepper; add enough water to mix to a firm dough. Knead gently on lightly floured surface until smooth; cover, refrigerate for 30 minutes.

Roll dough on lightly floured surface until 2mm thick. Prick all over with fork, cut into 4cm squares, place about 1cm apart onto greased oven trays. Brush with a little egg white, sprinkle with a little salt. Bake in moderate oven for about 15 minutes or until lightly browned; cool on trays.

Makes about 60.

LEFT: Cheese and Bacon Bites.
BELOW: From back: Fennel and Olive Pillows, Tomato Basil Crackers.

Below: China from Villeroy & Boch. Left: China and tray from Sydney Antique Centre

CHICKEN CRISPIES

1 cup plain flour
1 small chicken stock cube
60g butter
2 x 50g packets chicken-flavoured potato crisps, crushed
1 egg yolk
2 tablespoons milk, approximately
1 tablespoon milk, extra
2 tablespoons sesame seeds

Sift flour into bowl, rub in stock cube and butter. Stir in crisps, egg yolk and enough milk to make ingredients cling together. Knead gently on floured surface until smooth; cover, refrigerate for 30 minutes.

Roll dough between sheets of greaseproof paper until 5mm thick, cut into 5cm rounds, place about 2cm apart onto greased oven trays. Brush with extra milk; sprinkle with seeds. Bake in moderately hot oven for about 10 minutes or until lightly browned; cool on trays.

Makes about 45.

HERB AND GARLIC TRIANGLES

1 cup plain flour
½ teaspoon dry mustard
½ teaspoon garlic powder
90g butter
1 tablespoon chopped fresh parsley
1 tablespoon chopped fresh basil
1 tablespoon chopped fresh chives
½ cup grated tasty cheese
1 egg yolk

Sift dry ingredients into bowl, rub in butter. Stir in herbs, cheese and egg yolk, press mixture firmly together with hand. Knead gently on lightly floured surface until smooth; cover, refrigerate for 30 minutes.

Roll dough between sheets of greaseproof paper until 3mm thick. Cut dough into 4cm squares, then cut again to make triangles. Place triangles about 1cm apart onto greased oven trays. Bake in moderately hot oven for about 10 minutes or until lightly browned; cool on trays.

Makes about 100.

LEFT: From back: Chicken Crispies, Herb and Garlic Triangles.
Tiles from Country Floors

SOUR CREAM, GARLIC AND CHIVE CRISPS

1¾ cups plain flour
¼ cup self-raising flour
½ teaspoon salt
30g butter
½ cup sour cream
¼ cup chopped fresh chives
¼ cup water, approximately
2 egg yolks, lightly beaten
1 tablespoon garlic powder
1½ tablespoons onion flakes
⅓ cup grated fresh parmesan cheese

Sift flours and salt into bowl, rub in butter. Stir in sour cream, chives and enough water to make ingredients cling together. Knead on lightly floured surface until smooth; cover, refrigerate for 30 minutes.

Divide mixture into 6 portions. Roll 1 portion between sheets of greaseproof paper until 2mm thick. Place on greased oven tray, brush with a little egg yolk; sprinkle with about one-sixth of the combined garlic powder, onion flakes and cheese. Bake in moderately hot oven for about 10 minutes or until lightly browned. Lift onto wire rack to cool. Break into pieces when cold. Repeat with remaining dough, egg yolk and garlic mixture.

CHEESY CARROT CRACKERS

1½ cups plain flour
1 teaspoon dry mustard
125g butter
1 tablespoon cumin seeds
1 cup finely grated carrot
¾ cup grated tasty cheese
1 egg yolk

Sift flour and mustard into bowl, rub in butter. Stir in seeds, carrot, cheese and egg yolk, mix to a firm dough. Knead on lightly floured surface until smooth; cover, refrigerate for 30 minutes.

Roll dough on lightly floured surface until 3mm thick. Cut 5cm rounds from dough, place about 2cm apart onto greased oven trays. Bake rounds in moderately hot oven for about 12 minutes or until lightly browned; cool on trays.

Makes about 90.

BELOW: From left: Sour Cream, Garlic and Chive Crisps, Cheesy Carrot Crackers.
RIGHT: Blue Cheese Twists.
Below: Bowl from Amy's Tableware. Right: Flour bag from Appley Hoare Antiques

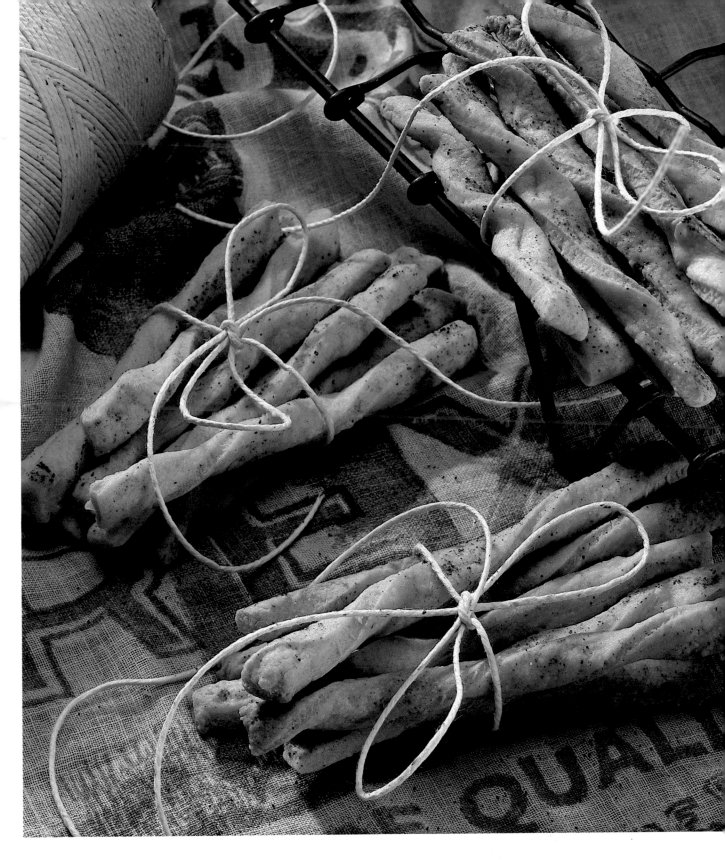

BLUE CHEESE TWISTS

1¼ cups plain flour
¼ cup self-raising flour
½ teaspoon salt
60g butter
125g firm blue vein cheese, grated
½ cup grated tasty cheese
1 egg yolk
3 teaspoons water, approximately
paprika

Sift flours and salt into bowl, rub in butter, stir in cheeses. Add egg yolk and enough water to make ingredients cling together. Knead gently on floured surface until smooth; cover, refrigerate for 30 minutes.

Roll dough between sheets of greaseproof paper into a rectangle about 3mm thick. Cut into 1cm x 10cm strips. Twist each strip, place about 2cm apart onto greased oven trays, sprinkle strips lightly with paprika. Bake in moderate oven for about 12 minutes or until lightly browned. Stand 5 minutes before lifting onto wire racks to cool.

Makes about 90.

SMOKED CHEESE
AND BACON STRAWS

1 teaspoon oil
4 bacon rashers, finely chopped
2 sheets ready rolled puff pastry
1 egg, lightly beaten
1 cup (125g) grated smoked cheese
2 green shallots, chopped
1 tablespoon chopped fresh parsley
1 teaspoon paprika

Heat oil in pan, add bacon, cook, stirring, until crisp; drain on absorbent paper. Brush pastry sheets with a little egg, sprinkle quarter of the cheese over half of each sheet, leaving 1cm border. Sprinkle with combined bacon, shallots, parsley, paprika and remaining cheese.

Fold sheets in half to enclose filling, press lightly together, brush surface with a little more egg. Cut crossways into 1cm strips, twist strips, place about 3cm apart onto greased oven trays. Bake in moderately hot oven for about 12 minutes or until lightly browned; cool on wire racks.

Makes about 40.

POPPY SEED PRETZELS

190g butter
1²⁄₃ cups plain flour
2 teaspoons lemon juice
²⁄₃ cup water, approximately
1 egg, lightly beaten
3 teaspoons poppy seeds
1 teaspoon paprika
pinch cayenne pepper
2 tablespoons grated parmesan
cheese
1 teaspoon salt

Have butter at room temperature. Sift flour into large bowl. Add juice and enough water to mix to a sticky dough. Knead on lightly floured surface for about 5 minutes or until smooth; cover dough, refrigerate for 15 minutes.

Place dough on lightly floured surface, cut a 2cm-deep cross into surface of dough. Pull corners of dough out to form a 4-leaf clover shape, about 36cm square.

Shape butter into a 12cm square block, place on centre of dough, fold flaps of pastry over each other to encase butter. Gently roll dough into 20cm x 40cm rectangle, fold over bottom third of dough, fold top third over bottom third; cover, refrigerate for 10 minutes.

Repeat rolling, folding and resting of dough 3 times, half turning the dough before rolling.

Roll dough into 20cm x 40cm rectangle, fold both ends over to meet in centre, fold in half; cover, refrigerate for 10 minutes. Repeat process.

Roll dough on lightly floured surface until 4mm thick, brush with a little of the egg, sprinkle with half the poppy seeds, then paprika, pepper and cheese. Cut dough into 1cm strips about 15cm long. Gently twist strips and loop into pretzel shapes. Brush uncut surfaces with more egg, sprinkle with remaining poppy seeds and salt. Place pretzels about 4cm apart onto greased oven trays, bake in hot oven for about 10 minutes or until puffed and lightly browned.

Makes about 60.

SPICED PUMPKIN
AND HAM SLICE

You will need about 350g uncooked pumpkin for this recipe.
1 cup plain flour
60g butter
1 egg yolk
2 tablespoons water, approximately
250g ham, finely chopped
TOPPING
2 teaspoons oil
1 clove garlic, crushed
½ teaspoon curry powder
½ teaspoon Chinese five
spice powder
½ teaspoon ground cumin
pinch chilli powder
1 cup cooked mashed pumpkin
1 tablespoon cornflour
1 egg, lightly beaten

Lightly grease 20cm x 30cm lamington pan, place strip of paper to cover base and extend over 2 opposite sides, grease paper. Sift flour into bowl, rub in butter; add egg yolk and enough water to give a firm dough. Knead gently on floured surface until smooth; cover dough, refrigerate for 30 minutes.

Roll pastry between sheets of greaseproof paper until large enough to cover base of prepared pan. Cover pastry with greaseproof paper, fill with dried beans or rice. Bake in moderately hot oven for 10 minutes, remove paper and beans, bake further 10 minutes or until lightly browned; cool.

Cook ham in small pan over high heat until crisp. Spread topping evenly over base, sprinkle with ham. Bake in moderate oven for about 15 minutes or until set.

Pumpkin Topping: Heat oil in pan, add garlic and spices, stir over heat for about 2 minutes; cool. Combine mashed pumpkin, cornflour and egg in bowl, stir in spice mixture.

RIGHT: Diamond shapes: Spiced Pumpkin and Ham Slice, Knot shapes: Poppy Seed Pretzels, Stick shapes: Smoked Cheese and Bacon Straws.

HINTS FOR SUCCESS

To obtain results like our luscious pictures, here are some guidelines to set you on the way. Our tips on mixing, baking and more will help you follow our recipes with confidence and enjoy cooking.

MIXING

For best results, have butter and eggs at room temperature. Do not over-beat butter and sugar mixtures. Over-beating will give a mixture which is excessively soft and can cause biscuits to spread too much during baking. Usually, it is best to stir in dry ingredients in 2 batches, often in a larger bowl.

OVEN TRAYS AND PANS

It is important to use the correct oven trays to ensure even baking and browning. We used flat aluminium trays which have little or no sides, to allow for proper heat circulation and browning.

Pictured is the Namco bakeware we used: clockwise from top: an oven tray, 20cm x 30cm lamington pan, 25cm x 30cm Swiss roll pan and 23cm square slab pan.

OVEN POSITIONS

Two or more trays of biscuits or pans of slices can be baked in an oven at the same time, provided the trays do not touch the oven sides or the oven door when it is closed.

There must be at least a 2cm space around each tray or pan to allow for proper heat circulation and browning.

For even cooking, change the position of trays or pans on the oven shelves halfway through baking. Some ovens have hot spots, and trays or pans need to be rotated as well, to help even browning.

As a general rule, if using a gas oven, the top half will give the best baking results. The lower half of an electric oven is best. Fan-forced ovens will bake and brown about 4 trays of biscuits at a time without changing shelf positions.

It is a good idea to check the oven manufacturer's instructions for finer details which apply to your oven.

TO TEST IF BISCUITS ARE COOKED

Our baking times are based on a minimum guide. Every oven differs slightly in temperature and may need checking for accuracy whether new or old.

Watch biscuits carefully during baking. Opening the oven door for short periods will not hurt the biscuits or slices.

Biscuits usually feel soft in the oven and become firmer or crisp when cold. A good test for most types of biscuits or cookies is to push a soft biscuit or cookie gently with the finger; if it can be moved on the tray without breaking, it is cooked.

Individual recipes state when it is necessary to cool on trays or if biscuits should be transferred to racks to cool.

TO TEST IF SLICES ARE COOKED

Slices and bases for layered slices usually feel slightly soft in the oven but become firm when cold.

TO STORE BISCUITS AND SLICES

To keep biscuits and slices fresh, choose containers which exclude as much air as possible. Biscuits and slices must be completely cold before storing, otherwise they will soften.

Biscuits and slices which are filled with jam or cream, etc., are best eaten the same day; fillings cause them to soften.

Biscuits and slices should not be stored with cakes, bread, scones, etc., as they will absorb moisture from these and will soften.

If plain biscuits or slices (unfilled and/or uniced) soften, place them on oven trays in a single layer and reheat, uncovered, in moderate oven for a few minutes to recrisp; lift onto wire racks to cool.

TO FREEZE BISCUITS AND SLICES

All baked biscuits, cookies and slices can be frozen successfully. However, some icings and cream fillings may crack or change in appearance on thawing and will not look like our photographs.

Always exclude as much air as possible from the container before freezing. Two months is about maximum freezing time. Uniced and unfilled biscuits or cookies may need to be re-crisped in single layers on oven trays in a moderate oven for a few minutes; cool on wire racks.

PIPING BAG ALTERNATIVE

In some recipes, we have used a piping bag to force out a mixture, but if you have a biscuit or cookie pusher you can use that instead. However, the thickness of biscuits and cookies will vary from ours and cooking times will also vary.

MICROWAVE OVEN COOKING

We did not cook any of these recipes in a microwave oven, as the result would be different from our photographs.

WHAT WENT WRONG

IF BISCUITS SPREAD ON THE TRAY: the mixture is too soft due to over-beating; ingredients have been measured incorrectly; incorrect flour has been used (such as self-raising when the recipe calls for plain flour); or the oven was not hot enough to set mixture quickly enough.

IF BISCUITS ARE TOO HARD: ingredients have been measured incorrectly; biscuits have been baked too long or at too high temperature; or incorrect type of oven trays have been used.

IF BISCUITS ARE TOO SOFT: they have not been cooked long enough, or have been stacked on top of each other to cool and have softened by steam.

IF BISCUITS ARE TOO BROWN UNDERNEATH: too much greasing has probably been used. We grease trays lightly and evenly with a little melted butter on a pastry brush. Excess greasing quickly attracts heat to base of biscuits. Incorrect oven position and temperature could also be the cause. Another could be excess sweetening, usually caused by over-generous measuring, particularly with ingredients such as sugar, honey or golden syrup.

GLOSSARY

Here are some terms, names and alternatives to help everyone use and understand our recipes perfectly.

ALCOHOL: is optional but gives a particular flavour. You can use fruit juice or water instead.

ALL-BRAN: a low-fat, high-fibre breakfast cereal based on wheat bran.

ALMOND PASTE: we used almond-flavoured cake paste or prepared marzipan.

ALMONDS, GROUND: use commercially ground nuts.

AMARETTO: an almond-flavoured liqueur.

BACON RASHERS: bacon slices.

BAKING POWDER: a raising agent consisting of an alkali and an acid. It is mostly made from cream of tartar and bicarbonate of soda in the proportions of 1 level teaspoon cream of tartar to ½ level teaspoon bicarbonate of soda. This is equivalent to 2 teaspoons baking powder.

BANANA CHIPS: sliced fried bananas.

BICARBONATE OF SODA: baking soda.

BISCUITS (cookies)

BUTTERNUT COOKIES: packaged plain biscuits containing oats, coconut, butter, etc.

KINGSTON: crunchy plain biscuits sandwiched with chocolate cream filling.

PLAIN CHOCOLATE: use unfilled chocolate biscuits.

SWEET: we used plain unfilled sweet biscuits.

TIM TAM: chocolate-coated layered chocolate biscuits with chocolate cream filling.

BUTTER: we used salted or unsalted (sweet) butter; 125g is equal to 1 stick butter.

CACHOUS: small round cake decorating sweets available in silver, gold or colours.

CAROB: is available in light and dark powder, also in block form.

CHOC BITS (morsels): buds of dark chocolate.

CHOC MELTS (compounded chocolate): are discs of dark compounded chocolate in 375g packets.

CHOCOLATE HAZELNUT SPREAD: Nutella.

CHOCOLATE TOPPING: a chocolate syrup used in milk drinks or on ice-cream.

CHOKITO BAR: chocolate-coated caramel fudge bar with crunchy rice crisps.

COCOA: cocoa powder.

COCONUT: use desiccated coconut unless otherwise specified. To toast: stir coconut in pan over heat until lightly browned.

CREAM: available in cans and cartons in supermarkets and Asian stores; coconut milk can be substituted, although it is thinner.

FLAKED: flaked and dried coconut flesh.

SHREDDED: thin strips of dried coconut. To toast: spread evenly onto oven tray, toast in moderate oven for about 5 minutes.

COFFEE AND CHICORY ESSENCE: a syrup based on sugar, caramel, coffee and chicory.

COFFEE SUBSTITUTE: we used Ecco.

COLOURINGS: we used concentrated liquid vegetable food colourings.

CORN FLAKES: breakfast cereal made from toasted corn.

CORNFLOUR: cornstarch.

CORNMEAL: polenta.

CREAM: we have specified thickened (whipping) cream when necessary; cream is simply a light pouring cream, also known as half 'n' half.

SOUR: a thick, commercially-cultured cream.

CRUNCHY OAT BRAN CEREAL: a low-fat, high-fibre toasted breakfast cereal

CUSTARD POWDER: pudding mix.

ESSENCE: an extract from fruit and flowers, used as a flavouring.

FIVE SPICE POWDER: a mixture of ground spices which include cinnamon, cloves, fennel, star anise and Szechwan pepper.

FLOUR

PLAIN: all-purpose flour.

SELF-RAISING: substitute plain (all-purpose) flour and baking powder in the proportion of ¾ metric cup plain flour to 2 level metric teaspoons of baking powder. If using 8oz cup, use 1 cup plain flour to 2 level teaspoons baking powder.

WHOLEMEAL PLAIN: wholewheat flour without the addition of baking powder.

WHOLEMEAL SELF-RAISING (WHOLEWHEAT): substitute plain wholemeal flour and baking powder as for self-raising flour.

FRUIT MEDLEY, DRIED: a dried fruit mixture containing apples, apricots, peaches, pears, sultanas and raisins.

FRUIT MINCE: also known as mincemeat.

GINGER

GLACE: fresh ginger root preserved in sugar syrup; crystallised ginger can be substituted; rinse off the sugar with warm water, dry ginger before using.

GROUND: powdered dried ginger root.

GRAND MARNIER: an orange-flavoured liqueur; Cointreau can be substituted.

HAWAIIAN FRUIT MIX: dried fruit mixture containing papaw, sultanas, pineapple, raisins, banana chips and coconut.

HAZELNUTS, GROUND: we used packaged commercially ground nuts.

JAM: a preserve of sugar and fruit.

JELLY CRYSTALS: fruit-flavoured gelatine crystals available from supermarkets.

LEMON BUTTER: lemon curd or cheese.

MALTED MILK POWDER: instant powdered product made from cow's milk, with extracts of malted barley and other cereals.

MILK: we used full-cream homogenised milk.

SWEETENED CONDENSED MILK: we used Nestle's milk which has 60 percent of the water removed, then sweetened with sugar.

MILK MELTS: are discs of compounded milk chocolate available in 375g packets.

MILO: a powdered food drink made from malt, milk solids, sugar, cocoa, etc.

MIXED PEEL: a mixture of crystallised citrus peel; also known as candied peel.

MUESLI: crunchy granola.

NATURAL: untoasted.

TOASTED: oil and honey added to natural muesli, then toasted.

NOUGAT, DESSERT: we used Callard & Bowser's dessert nougat.

NUTRI-GRAIN: breakfast cereal made from corn, oats and wheat.

OIL: use a light polyunsaturated salad oil.

PEANUT BUTTER: peanuts ground to a paste, available in crunchy and smooth.

PEPITAS: pumpkin seed kernels.

PEPPERMINT BOILED SWEETS, HARD: we used Molly Bushell's bull's eye sweets.

PICNIC BAR: chocolate-coated bar of peanuts, wafer, rice crisps and caramel.

PIE APPLE: canned apples for filling pies.

PUFF PASTRY: available from supermarkets in blocks and in ready-rolled sheets.

REDCURRANT JELLY: a preserve made from redcurrants; an imported product at supermarkets and delicatessens.

RICE BUBBLES: rice crispies.

RICE FLOUR: ground rice can be substituted.

RIND: zest.

ROSE FLOWER WATER (rosewater): an extract made from crushed rose petals.

RUM: we used an underproof dark rum.

SEMOLINA: hard part of the wheat, sifted out and used mainly for making pasta.

SESAME SEEDS: we used the white variety. To toast: spread seeds evenly onto oven tray, toast in moderate oven for about 5 minutes.

SCORCHED PEANUTS: chocolate-coated nuts.

SUGAR

BROWN: a soft fine-granulated sugar with molasses present.

CASTOR: fine granulated table sugar.

COFFEE CRYSTALS: large golden crystal sugar made to enhance coffee flavour.

CRYSTAL: granulated table sugar.

DEMERARA: small golden crystal sugar.

ICING: confectioners' or powdered sugar. We used icing sugar mixture, not pure, unless specified.

RAW: natural light brown granulated sugar or "sugar in the raw".

SULTANAS: seedless white raisins.

SUNFLOWER SEED KERNELS: the kernels of dried sunflower seeds.

SYRUP

LIGHT CORN: an imported product sold in supermarkets, delicatessens and health food stores.

GLUCOSE: also known as liquid glucose.

GOLDEN: a golden-coloured syrup made from sugar cane. Maple, pancake syrup or honey can be substituted.

MAPLE FLAVOURED: golden/pancake syrup; honey can be substituted.

VANILLA ESSENCE: we used imitation extract.

WEET-BIX: Weeta-bix or Ruskets.

WHITE MELTS: discs of compounded white chocolate available in 375g packets.

INDEX